ACKNOWLEDGEMENTS

First at all, I would like to thank my advisor, Dr. Fred J. Taylor, for his mentoring, patience, and friendship. The supports and resources he provided are unsurpassable and my appreciation to him is beyond words.

I would also like to thank Dr. Jose C. Principe, Dr. Herman Lam, Dr. Randy C.Y. Chow, and Dr. Jih-Kwon Peir for serving my committee.

Next, I would like to express my respect and thanks to the members in the HSDAL. They all were great to work with and full of energy and good ideas. Special thanks goes to Dr. Ahmad R. Ansari for the pioneer works he did for the Osculant project. I would also like to thank Dr. Uwe and Anke Meyer-Bäse for the supports and advice they gave me.

I would like to thank my parents, whose love, sacrifice, encouragement, and ultimate support made my degree possible. Finally, I have to thank my lovely wife, Yi-miao. She made my Ph.D. years both exciting and enjoyable.

TABLE OF CONTENTS

Abstract of Dissertation Presented to the Graduate School
of the University of Florida in Partial Fulfillment of the
Requirements for the Degree of Doctor of Philosophy

OSCULANT:
A SELF-ORGANIZING SCHEDULING AND RESOURCE MANAGEMENT
SCHEME IN A NETWORK COMPUTING ENVIRONMENT

By

Hsin-Ho Wu

December 1998

Chairman: Dr. Fred J. Taylor
Major Department: Electrical and Computer Engineering

In this dissertation, a new scheduling scheme called Osculant is studied. The
Osculant scheduler is bottom-up, self-organized, and designed for distributed
heterogeneous computing systems. In the first part of the dissertation, performance
evaluations of uniform latency communication (UCL) and non-uniform latency
communication (NUCL) networks are performed. By studying the analytical model and
simulation results of UCL networks, we found that network performance can be
predictable if the job arrival rate is known in advance. However, UCL networks' high cost
growth rate prohibits it from being applied in general distributed computing systems.
Conversely, NUCL networks are more scalable and economical but are more difficult to
predict the communication performance. Studies show that locality properties are the keys
to improve performance of NUCL systems. In the Osculant, we develop new techniques

in exploiting localities embedded in the applications and systems.

Several new dynamic bidding strategies were introduced and investigated. Compared to the top-down scheduling scheme, the performance-bidding and energy-based bidding methods improve the system throughput rate and average job energy consumption rate. Multiple-bid methods are developed to further improve the performance of single-bid strategies (e.g., the performance- and energy-based bidding methods). *Dynamic Jobpost Bidding Model* and *Resource Contractor Bidding Model* are the two examples of this category. Experimental results show very promising performance growth over the single-bid methods. It is also found that system ethos can be altered to suit the user demands and environmental changes by choosing different bidding methods. Moreover, with multiple-bid methods, system status information is progressively gathered through multiple job announcement and bidding processes. It is shown that scheduling overheads can be effectively reduced by this scheme.

The Osculant Job Profile Generator (JPG) generates job profiles on-line so that other nodes can estimate resource requirements and job completion cost. The Multi-layer Jobpost Protocol (MJP) is developed to announce jobs to the computing system. The MJP is found to be robust and self-regulated. Studies of other modules in the Osculant Shell reveal even more potential of the Osculant scheduling scheme.

CHAPTER 1
INTRODUCTION

1.1 Motivation

Heterogeneous network computing is now ubiquitous and is found in virtually every major computing environment. Heterogeneous computing is known to be cost-effective, robust, and scaleable. With Moore's law [Schaller 1997] driving technological improvements, the entire field of heterogeneous computing is undergoing a metamorphosis. Nevertheless, within this dynamically changing landscape, there is a need to provide management of these computational resources. Computer engineers unknowingly have, for some time, been introducing market driven philosophies into their design strategies. These include organization theory (e.g., shared resources), recycling (e.g., cache), commodity investment (e.g., speculative computing), to name but a few. Current studies have indicated that market driven concepts can, in fact, be integrated formally into a resource management and scheduling paradigms for heterogeneous computing systems. What important to realize is that network computing suffers from the same set of restrictions that govern supply-side economics in terms of access to resources and services and hierarchical control. These system-level attributes and resources, which are important to the conducted study, relate to

● Bandwidth and latency: It is self-evident that network bandwidth restrictions can seriously impair timely execution tasks. Another performance limiting observation is

1

that network latency (i.e., the time required to receive requested information) is not directly correlated to communication bandwidth when the message lengths are small.

- Localized information and service providers: In order to avoid unnecessary network traffic congestion, information storage should be distributed, or duplicated, in a prudent manner. In this way, a balance is achieved between system performance and system cost.

These observations point out that task and resource scheduling will play an important role in improving the performance of virtually any network-based computing environment. A new bottom-up resource scheduling paradigm, call Osculant, was proposed as an innovative facilitating technology.

1.2 Dissertation Outline and Summary

In this dissertation, we investigate a new scheme that will schedule tasks and allocate resources in a bottom-up fashion within a distributed computing system. We demonstrate, through analytical modeling of network traffic and a series of simulations, how different scheduling policies accommodate changing system status, conditions, and job input rate. We also built a prototype scheduler with job profile generator, job announcing, and bidding processes to see how such a paradigm works in a real computing system. The remainder of this dissertation is organized as follows.

Chapter 2 serves as the background and presents material that will act as a foundation for the dissertation. We first explain the target environment of this research. Then, related studies in qualifying network performance, load balancing, task scheduling, and resource management are reviewed.

Chapter 3 presents the overview of the Osculant scheduling scheme. First, we explain the basic ideas and logical operation of the Osculant scheduler. Next, the Osculant simulator and job state transition are introduced. The third part reports the initial performance studies based on the Osculant scheduling scheme. Here, we compare the Osculant to several top-down scheduling schemes.

In Chapter 4, a network performance study based on the analytical model of multiple stage interconnection networks is presented. We first study the analytical model and learn how the network performance index can be extracted. Then, an original simulator is presented that is used to verify the correctness of the analytical model. By comparing the two, we learn how job input rate, network configuration, and network scaling affect the overall system performance. In the next part, we extend our scope to non-uniform communication latency (NUCL) networks that are used in most distributed systems. In this study, we exploit the locality issues in NUCL networks.

Chapter 5 presents the mechanisms of the Osculant scheduling scheme. First, jobpost distribution protocols are discussed. Next, various bidding strategies and simulation results are analyzed. Later, the resource management scheme in the Osculant is explained.

Chapter 6 demonstrates the development of the Osculant shell. The Osculant Job Profile Generator is presented and results are discussed. Remainder of this chapter discusses the other parts of the prototype scheduler.

In Chapter 7, we conclude the dissertation with a summary of the research results presented. Possible future research directions are also discussed.

CHAPTER 2
BACKGROUND

2.1 Target Environment

In this dissertation, the Osculant scheduling scheme will be studied. The target of the Osculant scheme is a general-purpose distributed heterogeneous computing environment. To achieve optimal system performance for such a computing environment, the system can have an assumed central node that has knowledge of the status of all nodes. Obviously, there are too many obstacles to realize such a system even without considering the aspects in scaling and reliability. In Osculant, we exploit the bottom-up approach that can self-organize the system driven by user demands and system conditions. Our goal is to improve the overall system performance and exploit the benefits of scalability and reliability nature from the bottom-up approach.

A distributed computing system can be described by the following components: working nodes, network configuration, jobs and applications, and management policies. A working node is defined as a device that is capable of job processing or resource management. They can be mainframe computers, workstations, file servers, personal computers, and even portable computers. Because working nodes not only vary in their performance and architecture but also change their states in timely basis, the developing scheme must have the ability to collect or probe the system states and nature of jobs. In

4

the dissertation, a working node is characterized by its computation power, memory size, storage capacity, and type of architecture.

Network configuration is rather flexible for the target computing environment. The goal of our studies is to develop a scheduling scheme that can be applied to systems without regarding their underlying connection structure. That is, the communication scheme under our studies will be topology-independent. In the dissertation, each node in the target system has a fixed degree of connections and point-to-point connections are used to link them. Data transmissions are accomplished by packet switching where data are divided into many small packets before transmission. It is assumed that each node has finite amount of buffers and will reject new packets when its buffer is full. Paths between the source and destination nodes are always the shortest in terms of the number of intermediate nodes passed. However, there may be more than one shortest path between any two nodes in the system.

Allowed job types are reasonably flexible. In contrast to real-time systems, which allow only well-known jobs, new jobs are allowed to enter the system because completion time constraints are not the top priority goal in the target environment. Jobs can be generated by any participating nodes and need to access remote file servers and databases for appropriate services and resources. It is also assumed that jobs are allowed to be executed at remote nodes for performance considerations. Finally, jobs in the target environment are assumed to be run in batch mode, i.e. information required to execute the job must be fixed prior to the scheduling phase. Typical jobs for the target environment include engineering applications, medical image processing, and scientific research programs. In the following sections, issues and problems that we encountered will be discussed. Also, related studies and researches will be reviewed.

2.2 Network Traffic Studies

In many cases, the network performance determines the overall capabilities of a distributed computing system. Overall system performance can be discussed in two categories: The first category, network performance, is determined by two important metrics: user response time and network utilization. The response time of a networked system can be related to many factors. For example, network configuration and number of active users will affect the response time. Studies [Blommers 1996] show that response time is independent of the number of users as long as the resource utilization remains low; and it is linear to the number of users when the utilization is near *100%*. Network utilization and throughput can also be affected by many factors. For instance, data segment size and network roundtrip time can be directly related to network throughput performance. Because data segment size, which is governed by the size of packets and maximum transmit unit (MTU) setting, is fixed under various standards, streaming capable transport protocols like TCP can improve the throughput rate by continuously sending data into the network before receiving acknowledgements.

The second category is the cost to build and maintain the network. It is important to correctly evaluate the requirements of current users and predict possible future growth. The degree of network provisioning and profitability of network investment must be on a proper ratio or the network performance or maintenance cost will be deteriorated. When a system is saturated, one has to decide whether to upgrade the servers or to install more servers. Generally speaking, component upgrades are cheaper but two servers are more reliable than one. So, the solution depends on the system and user requirements. For instance, we can bring the resource servers closer to their users by duplicating or moving the resources. On the other hand, queuing theory tells us that one fast server is better than two half speed servers because both cases give about the same performance while the fast server case has better response time performance in a lightly loaded condition.

A node in a distributed computing system is either a client or a server. When the network performance is concerned, the location of nodes is the most important factor. In is clear that clients located on the same local-area network (LAN) as their servers will get the best performance. So, one can bring the data closer to the client by either move the data onto a local server or move the remote server to the client-side LAN. This solution may not be appealing to users located at other locations because it may increase the network delays they see. The classic way to solve this problem is to conduct a network-wide traffic matrix study to determine location, number, and traffic load for all client systems. Observations also show that client-server applications tend to be the least sensitive to network delays because they are already incur processing delays on both sides, and this masks the network delay to some extent.

Network performance can be modeled and evaluated by mathematical modeling and simulations. Numerous research studies have been conducted in this filed. For example, Patel [Patel 1981] examined the operation and performance of crossbars and delta networks. Yoon et al. [Yoon 1990] followed Patel's study and extended it to switch-based networks with multiple buffers. However, as the system and network configurations become more complex, it is extremely difficult to model them. Analytical models generally make assumptions on the job arrival rate and system service rate, and their results are derived for a steady-state condition that is rarely observed in general network systems. By keeping these arguments in mind, we review the studies of Patel and Yoon et al. closely in Chapter 4 since they can be used to study the network performance of our target environment under certain conditions.

The importance of client/server allocations has been explained early in this section. In this dissertation, two manifestations of this idea will be explored. First, the distributed scheduling scheme will try to find the best processing node based on job contents and system status; and second, we will explore the technique to dynamically relocate servers and resources in a distributed system to achieve better performance.

2.3 Load Balancing Algorithms

Load balancing and resource allocation are key topics in designing efficient multiple-node systems. Load balancing algorithms try to improve system performance by redistributing the workload submitted by users. Early studies focus on static placement techniques that seek optimal or near optimal solutions to processor or resource allocation. Solution methods of this category contain graph theoretic approaches, mathematical programming, and queuing theory [Goscinski 1991]. Recent research in this field evolved to adaptive load balancing with process migration [Goscinski 1991]. A simple manifestation of this method is to have a central allocation processor that receives periodically load information from all processors and then makes process placement decisions. The central processor, however, can become a single point of failure and a bottleneck of the system.

Distributed process allocation algorithms become a complex alternative. A good example of distributed load balancing which is conceptually similar to Osculant is the microeconomic algorithm by Ferguson et al. [Ferguson 1988]. In this model, all processors and tasks are independent economic agents who attempt to selfishly optimize their satisfaction. All agents have to obey the rules set for the system to achieve their goals. That is, according to the economy model, job agents have to pay for CPU and network services based on their budget, and processor agents sell CPU time and communication bandwidth with the price depend on the demands. The processor agents have to advertise their price on bulletin boards in neighboring nodes so that job agents can shop around for best suited services.

The reported load balancing algorithms are generally designed either for closely coupled system or for homogeneous systems. With the advent of loosely coupled heterogeneous computing systems, more considerations will be required to improve the overall system performance.

2.4 Task Scheduling Algorithms

According to Goscinski [Goscinski 1991], a distributed scheduling policy can be divided into two components, namely

- a local scheduler that decides how to distribute the computation time of a processor to its resident processes, and
- a load distributing strategy that distributes the system load among the computing nodes.

The designs of local schedulers are generally simpler, for example, round-robin, priority queue, and time-slice policies are frequently used in existing operation systems. In designing local scheduler, fairness and priority are usually the most important issues.

On the other hand, load distribution strategies concentrate on improving system performance by sharing and balancing the system load. It is easy to observe that, in distributed systems, load sharing, load balancing, resource allocation, and task scheduling are closely related. In the Osculant, a bottom-up approach is employed. That is, system status has to be known by either a collection or a probing process before a task can be assigned or a resource can be allocated. Many studies can be related to the Osculant scheduling scheme. In the state-collection category, Shin and Chang [Shin 1988, 1995] proposed a resource allocation policy that uses *buddy sets* to reduce the state-collection overhead in a multicomputer configuration similar to our target environment. For the state-probing category, task announcement and bidding processes were first introduced by Smith [Smith 1980] in his *contract net protocol* that facilitates distributed control of cooperative task execution. Focused addressing techniques were also introduced by Smith in an effort to reduce network traffic. A good example that follows Smith's approach is done by Ramamritham and Stankovic [Ramamritham 1989, 1994]. In their studies, a distributed task scheduler with real-time constraints and resource requirement was studied. An effort to maximize the guarantee ratio in meeting completion time constraints is accomplished by *focused addressing* and *bidding* techniques. Nodes have to calculate the *surplus*, i.e. the bids, of processing the announced task. In turn, the parent node uses previously collected surplus information to limit the scope of the task announcing process or even award tasks according to the surplus information to accelerate the scheduling time. By combining focused addressing and bidding algorithms, Ramamritham and Stankovic introduced the *flexible algorithm* that allows a two-level task announcing/bidding structure to shorten the scheduling delay and improve the system performance. Blake and Schwan [Blake 1991] and Ni et al. [Ni 1985] also performed bottom-up scheduling studies using various bidding strategies. These task scheduling schemes, however, are restricted to hard real-time environments where most of the task and resource requirements are well known prior to the scheduling time. Overall system performance such as utilization is generally neglected.

Comparing to the reported bottom-up task scheduling studies, the Osculant scheduling scheme exploits the *state-probing* approach with *self-regulating task announcement* processes and aggressive *bidding* strategies. Improving system performance in a general-purpose distributed computing environment, where execution time constraints are not critical and new tasks are allowed to enter the system, is the main mission. In addition, the Osculant scheduling scheme is flexible, fault-tolerable, and scalable because of the nature of the bottom-up approach.

2.5 Resource Management Schemes

According to Goscinski [Goscinski 1991], resources are reusable and relatively stable hardware or software components of a computer system that are useful to system users or to their processes. Because of their usefulness, they are requested, used, and released by processes during their activities. Resources also can be grouped as low-level resources and high-level resources. Low-level resources can be used directly by the distributed system and users. However, high-level resources, which are built upon several low-level resources, are more commonly utilized in the system. Hardware resources are generally static, permanent, and limited in quantity. Management of physical resources is simpler than logical resources because the latter may be varied temporally and quantitatively.

Software resources can be pre-defined by the system or composed by the users. They can also be active (so that they can change states), or static. Furthermore, advances in network computing and in software engineering bring both new opportunities and problems to the management of logical resources. For instance, software components will be required to be managed properly in a heterogeneous system with differences in suitability for the underlying platforms and in service quality. In other words, multiple software versions and locations may coexist that can be used and/or retrieved to complete the task with differing costs and functionality. Additionally, as purchasing and maintenance of software becomes more dominant in the overall operation cost of computing systems, licensing and revision control will become an important topic in the future resource management.

The software industry has begun to adapt the "thin-client," "component software," and "just-in-time application" concepts. "Fat-clients" are difficult to manage, and they add to network congestion. On the other hand, in the "thin-clients" environment, applications are stored and managed centrally on servers. Appropriate executables and data files (logical resources) are sent and stored in local caches when needed.

Castanet [Thomas 1997] and *ALTiS* [Goulde 1997] are two pioneer systems built on the thin-client concepts to distribute Java applications. Corel Corp. tried and demonstrated some of the WordPerfect suite (*Corel Office JV*) in their Java implementation so that applications can be launched and executed from web browsers on different platforms. *ComponentWare* [ComponentWare 1997], by I-Kinetics Inc., is a design based on Common Object Request Broker Architecture (COBRA) that integrates customer applications from prefabricated software components. These trends suggest that software resources are changing. Existing scheduling and resource management methods may be inefficient to handle them.

Traditionally, resource allocations are done centrally by schedulers with queue or priority schemes. As the types and number of computing resource grow, it will be more difficult to efficiently manage the resources in centralized approaches. Therefore, many distributed resource management schemes were developed. For example, in agent based resource management schemes [Goscinski 1991], the policy of accessing resources is enforced by the resource owners. An agent process has to be created at both the client and server. The local agent searches and borrows resources from the remote agent, and the remote agent verifies the borrowing request and provides the service. Another example can be seen from the study performed by Gagliano et al. [Gagliano 1995]. In their approach, a free-market principle was used to allocate computing resources. Tasks are given an initial fund to acquire needed resources and they have to bid on resources offered by the system. An auction process is convened by all the waiting tasks when a task arrived or is completed. Their studies show that decentralized approaches are more flexible and have better reaction time.

In this dissertation, we approach this problem by a combination of agent and free-market approaches. That is, we allow intermediate nodes to store and provide the logical resources to other nodes. We established a scheme that merges the scheduling and resource management processes so that the overhead is reduced. We also show that, with

some extensions, our scheme can accommodate the thin-client structure.

CHAPTER 3
OVERVIEW OF THE OSCULANT SCHEDULER

3.1 Basis of The Osculant Scheduling Scheme

Osculant differs from existing task and resource scheduling paradigms in that it is bottom-up and self-organizing. Experimental studies have led to the conclusion that Osculant is: (1) architecturally robust, (2) capable of internalizing the management of system assets, and (3) able to dynamically alter the system ethos to range from a real-time operation, to maximize bandwidth, to minimize latency, to minimize energy dissipation. The Osculant paradigm can be motivated as follows

- An Osculant system consists of a collection of possibly dissimilar autonomous information systems (e.g., capabilities, instruction set, local storage, I/O) which may or may not be connected by a network with an arbitrary topology and time- and space-varying behavior.

- Executed programs send messages to a higher level entity, called the *steward*, which interprets these requests in terms of executable objects and posts them on a *job board* along with salient information about data location, resource requirements, job priority, and so forth.

- When a job is posted, all processors bid on that job in a manner that maximizes their profit (measured in terms of tangibles such as net number of cycles per unit time). Job bids are a function of processor resources, locality of data, I/O costs, job priority,

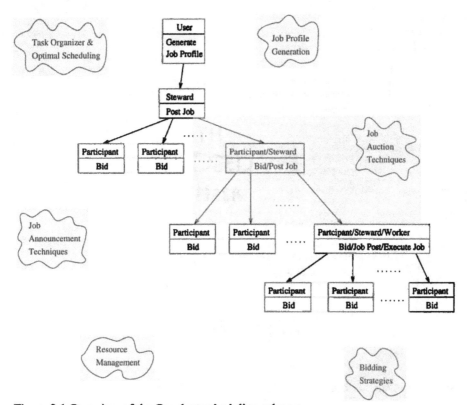

Figure 3.1 Overview of the Osculant scheduling scheme.

existing local job queue, and so forth. Processors have no knowledge of other bids and operate autonomously. The *steward* receives bids and awards tasks to the processor with the best bid.

● Any processor can play one of the three following roles:

1. *User*: A user node issues jobs.

2. *Steward*: A *steward* node manages jobs authorized by other users or assigned by *stewards*.

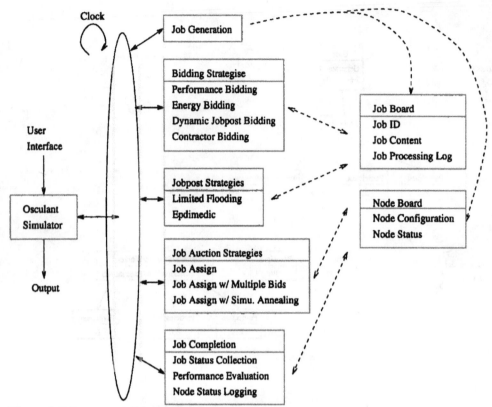

Figure 3.2 Structure of the Osculant Simulator.

3. *Participant*: A participant node bids jobs and executes the job once assigned by
   the *steward*.

● Role assignments of nodes are based on individual jobs and circumstances. Hence, a

node can play one or more roles at the same time for different jobs.

Figure 3.1 shows an example of the basic operations of the Osculant scheduler and

the related study areas. It should be noted that Figure 3.1 only shows the logical

hierarchical structure of the Osculant system. In reality, the connection scheme can be

graph, ring, tree, or a combination of them.

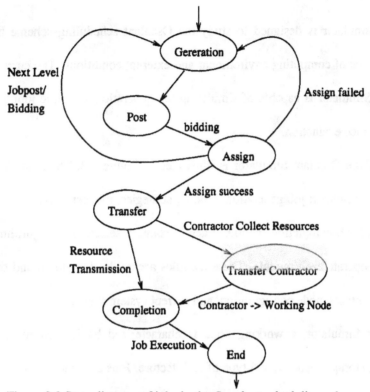

Figure 3.3 State diagram of jobs in the Osculant scheduling scheme.

The basic market-driven philosophy underlying an Osculant system is a competitive bidding scheduling scheme. The key to successful bidding is to estimate accurately and efficiently the cost-complexity of a posted job. This is the role of the job profile generator (JPG). Job profiles are first generated from the information provided by the tasks that are distributed among participating nodes. Upon receiving the job profiles, the distributed heterogeneous nodes calculate the completion cost of a task based on their interests, ethos, biases, and capabilities. A job will be assigned to the node by the *steward* (which is re-locatable) with best bid.

3.2 The Osculant Simulator

The Osculant Simulator is designed to study the Osculant scheduling scheme by simulating various types of computing environment and external conditions. The current version of Osculant Simulator is capable of simulating job generation, dynamic jobpost, bidding, and performance evaluation.

The structure of the Osculant Simulator is illustrated in Figure 3.2. There are five major modules in the simulator: job generation, bidding strategies, jobpost strategies, job auction strategies, and job completion module. Each contains a selection of algorithms and subroutines that operate each module. These modules access the Job Board and the Node Board for job contents, node configuration, and current system status.

In the Osculant Simulator, a working node is characterized by its computation power, memory size, storage capacity, and type of architecture. Jobs are managed locally by the local scheduler in a node. In most cases, jobs are processed in the order of job arrival time, and a first-in-first-out (FIFO) queue is maintained for the waiting jobs. In a later part of the dissertation, a non-preemptive local scheduler was implemented to improve the node utilization. In order to reduce the complexity, it is further assumed a node cannot process jobs with requirements that exceed the node's physical limitations, e.g. memory size, and jobs from different architectures, e.g. no software emulators.

As mentioned in Chapter 2, data transmissions are accomplished using packet switching techniques. It is assumed that each node has a finite amount of buffers and shortest paths will be chosen to route the packets. In order to simplify the analysis, virtual-circuit packet switching [Stallings 1986] is used to route the packets between the source and destination nodes. This means that a route between two nodes is set up prior to data transmission. This route is not a dedicated path and may change every time. Packets follow the same route and are buffered at each node. Blocking may happen in the intermediate nodes and packets are queued for output over a line.

The Osculant Simulator is implemented with the time-advance concept that scans all modules for events at each time step. Initial events, which contain job generation time, locations, resource requirements, and resource locations, node configurations, and network bandwidth, are generated using a MATLAB program with user-defined statistical models. Internal states of jobs and nodes are created and are inserted by the simulator during run-time. State diagram of jobs is shown in Figure 3.3.

The current version of Osculant Simulator is implemented by using C language and is executed on UNIX environments (tested on SUN OS, HP-UX, and LINUX). Appendix C illustrates the Osculant Simulator user interface. The simulation configuration file allows users to change a wide range of system parameters such as: job contents, node configurations, network configurations, bidding strategies, jobpost protocols, resource management schemes, and other system parameters.

3.3 Initial Performance Studies on the Osculant Scheduling Scheme

The Osculant is a bottom-up scheme that is capable of assimilating the most up-to-date system information and, therefore, achieves near-optimal scheduling performance. Performance improvement is attained with the possible overhead expense associated with a relatively long time period spent in jobpost/bidding process. In this section, the characteristics of jobpost/bidding delay on the system performance are studied.

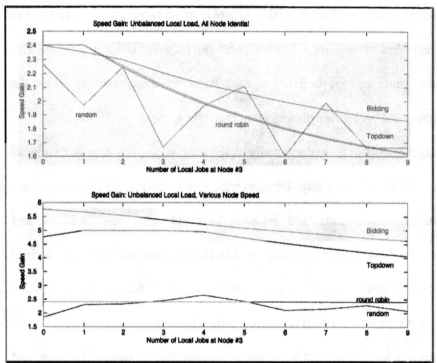

Figure 3.3 Comparisons between top-down schedulers and the bidding scheme. In these results, the bidding scheme outperforms the top-down schemes when the system load becomes unbalanced. The bidding scheme has more prominent performance advantages when the system contains processors with diverse service rate.

In order to show the effects of jobpost/bidding delays, three top-down schemes are compared to the Osculant bidding scheme:

- Round robin: Jobs are assigned to working nodes in a sequential order among working nodes.

- Random: Jobs are distributed randomly among the working nodes.

- Well informed top-down scheduler: The scheduler has complete knowledge about the capabilities of all working nodes but does not have information about the load generated locally at the nodes. This scheme also serves as an ideal comparison counterpart to the bidding scheme because it accurately estimates working node information without any jobpost/bidding delay if there is a lack of local activity at every processor.

The results are retrieved from a sequence of simulations. In the simulator, a collection of jobs is generated and fed into the scheduler with various local loads (jobs that are generated by local users which are unpredictable to the top-down scheduler) and system parameters (that are known to the schedulers). Jobs are characterized by job size, and by similarities between jobs and job generation rate.

The first simulation results shown in Figure 3.3 assume a homogeneous system with four identical processors. Local jobs are added gradually to one of the working processors while they keep the local load of other nodes constant. The results show that the performance gain of random scheduler remains random; the round robin scheduler and the well informed top-down scheduler have approximately the same performance; the Osculant scheduler gradually performs better as the level of unbalanced load is increased. These results show that the Osculant scheme can adapt effectively to the current processor status under this condition. The effect of post/bidding overhead also can be observed from this figure: When the homogeneous system is well balanced and lightly loaded, both the round robin scheduler and the well informed top-down scheduler outperform the bidding scheme.

The same simulation is also performed in a heterogeneous system of four processors with different service rates (*1:2:3:4* in this example). Simulation is achieved by manipulating the local job load as in the homogeneous case. As shown by the results, the advantage of the Osculant scheme becomes more prominent. In this case, both the

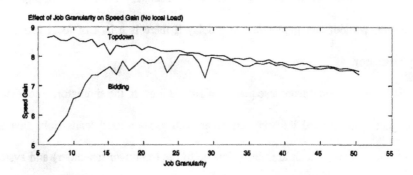

Figure 3.4 The effect of job granularity on the performance of bidding scheme. The performance of the top-down scheduler is an ideal case counterpart if the jobpost/bidding delay is not present.

random and round-robin schedulers have worse performance while the Osculant scheduler generally outperforms the well-informed top-down scheduler by around *20%*. This is mainly because the bidding scheme can retrieve more accurate local information than the top-down schemes. When the well-known top-down scheduler distributes a job to a heavily loaded processor, the performance penalty to the system is more severe in a heterogeneous system than in a homogeneous system.

The simulation reported in Figure 3.4 investigates how the jobpost/bidding overheads affect the overall system performance. In this simulation, the well-informed top-down scheduler has accurate knowledge of the working node status and lacks a local job load in the working nodes. Under this condition, the quality of job distribution by the host processor is comparable to the bidding scheme but lacks bidding overhead. Therefore, the well-informed top-down scheduler serves as an ideal case for the Osculant scheduler. The other parameter under control is the job granularity. Here, a job is partitioned into different sizes and the overall completion time is measured. From the results, as job granularity increases, performance of bidding scheme gradually approaches the ideal top-down scheduler. Conversely, large job granularity will result in low performance gain because of low degree of parallelism.

These studies suggest that Osculant can perform as well as the best top-down scheduler, as well as offering its unique properties and attributes. In the next chapter, network performance of distributed computing systems will be studied to identify the key components of the proposed scheduling scheme.

CHAPTER 4
ANALYTICAL NETWORK PERFORMANCE MODELS

4.1 Introduction

The communication schemes in multiprocessor systems play an important role in determining the overall system performance. The fundamental of the network performance model is based on the studies from uniform communication latency (UCL) interconnection networks [Johnson 1992]. The UCL network model can be applied to study various types of communication schemes among computing nodes. In this chapter, an analytical model is studied and verified by a simulator so that a better cost-to-performance ratio can be found with customized requirements.

Based on the studies on UCL networks, we extend our range to non-uniform communication latency (NUCL) interconnection networks [Johnson 1992], which are used in most distributed computing systems. From these studies and observations, an understanding of communications in a heterogeneous computing environment can be obtained and applied in the Osculant study.

4.2 Basic Concepts of Switch-Based Networks

The basic element of switch-based networks is a crossbar switch as shown in Figure 4.1 with various sizes from 2x2 to a larger system. Assume that m is the probability that a source node issues a request during a cycle into an M-by-N crossbar switch. Patel [Patel

Figure 4.1 *MxN* crossbar switch.

1981] shows that the bandwidth, which is the number of requests that arrive at the destination node during this cycle, is

$$BW = N * (1 - (1 - m/N)^M)$$ (1)

and the normalized throughput rate of the *M-by-N* crossbar switch is

$$P = BW/(m*M)$$ (2)

It is well known that the cost of a crossbar switch is $O(n^2)$ to its size. Therefore, it is impractical to use single crossbar switch to connect all nodes in a distributed system. So, a multistage interconnection network (MIN) is used to interconnect a large number of nodes by using many small crossbar switches. The performance of MINs varies according to the number of switching elements (SEs) as well as the topology of connecting crossbar switches.

4.3 Performance Model of Multiple Stage Interconnection Networks

In this section, the performance model of a typical uniform communication latency (UCL) interconnection network, the delta network, is reviewed and investigated. An *N*-by-*N* delta network consists of $\left\lfloor \dfrac{N}{a} \right\rfloor$ *n* *a-by-a* crossbar switches, where $N = a^n$. A packet movement through the network can be controlled locally at each switching element (SE)

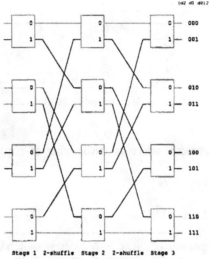

(d2 d1 d0)2

000
001

010
011

100
101

110
111

Stage 1   2-shuffle   Stage 2   2-shuffle   Stage 3

Figure 4.2 The 8x8 delta network.

by a single base-a digit of the destination address of the packet. Figure 4.2 shows an *8x8*

delta network by using *12 2x2* crossbar switches.

Following the study by Yoon et al. [Yoon 1990], the analytical model is built based

on the following assumptions:

(1) Packets are generated at each node with equal probability, and the arrivals of

packets are memoryless.

(2) Packets are directed uniformly over all network outputs.

(3) The routing logic at each SE is fair, i.e. conflicts are randomly resolved.

These assumptions imply that the distribution of packets is uniform and statistically

independent for all SEs. Consider the single buffer case and the state diagram in Figure

4.3 where $q(k,t)$ is the probability that a packet is ready to come to a buffer of an SE at

stage k during t_{th} stage cycle; $r(k,t)$ is the probability that a packet in a buffer of an SE at

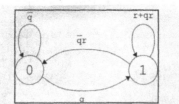

Figure 4.3 Transition diagram of single buffer MINs.

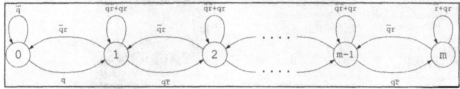

Figure 4.4 The state transition diagram of multi-buffer MINs.

stage k is able to move forward during t_{th} stage cycle giving that there is a packet in the buffer. Then we have

$$q(k,t) = 1 - (1 - P_1(k-1,t)/a)^a. \tag{3}$$

where $P_1(k,t)$ is the probability that a buffer of an SE at stage k is full at the beginning of the t_{th} stage cycle, and $P_0(k,t)$ is the probability that a buffer is empty. Then,

$$r(k,t) = r'(k,t) * (P_0(k+1,t) + P_1(k+1,t)*r(k+1,t)) \tag{4}$$

$$q(k+1,t) = P_1(k,t) * r'(k,t) \tag{5}$$

$$r'(k,t) = q(k+1,t) / P_1(k,t) \tag{6}$$

where $r'(k,t)$ is the probability that a packet of an SE at stage k can move to the output of the SE during the t_{th} stage cycle giving that there is a packet in the buffer. Since $q(1,t)$ is the probability that there is a packet coming to a buffer at first stage during a cycle, it is the arrival rate of a single input port of the network. Finally, according to the state diagram shown in Figure 4.3, we have

$$P_0(k,t) = P_0(k,t)(1-q(k,t)) + P_1(k,t)*(1-q(k,t))*r(k,t) \tag{7}$$

$$P_1(k,t) = P_0(k,t)*q(k,t) + P_1(k,t)*[q(k,t)*r(k,t) + (1-r(k,t))] \qquad (8)$$

Similarly, Yoon et al. expanded the model to multiple buffer delta networks with following additional definitions:

m : Buffer size.

$P_j(k,t)$: Probability that there are j packets in a buffer of an SE at stage k at the beginning of the t_{th} stage cycle.

$P_0(k,t)$: Probability that there is no packet in the buffer.

$(1-P_0(k,t))$: Probability that the buffer is not empty.

$P_m(k,t)$: Probability that the buffer is full.

$(1-P_m(k,t))$: Probability that the buffer is not full.

Using the modified state diagram in Figure 4.4, we get the same equation pairs as in a single buffered delta network.

$$q(k,t) = 1-[1-(1-P_0(k-1,t)/a)^a \qquad 2 \le k \le n \qquad (9)$$

$$r(k,t) = [q(k+1,t)*(1-P_0(k,t)]*[1-P_m(k+1,t)+ P_m(k+1,t)*r(k+1,t)]$$

$$1 \le k \le n-1 \qquad (10)$$

$$r(n,t) = q(n+1,t)/(1-P_0(n,t)) \qquad (11)$$

$$P_j(k,t+1) = q(k,t)*[P_{j-1}(k,t)*(1-r(k,t)+P_j(k,t)*r(k,t)]$$

$$+(1-q(k,t))*[P_j(k,t)*(1-r(k,t)+P_{j+1}(k,t)*r(k,t)]$$

$$2 \le j \le m-1, 1 \le k \le n \qquad (12)$$

$$P_0(k,t+1) = (1-q(k,t))*[P_0(k,t) + P_1(k,t)*r(k,t)] \qquad 1 \le k \le n \qquad (13)$$

$$P_1(k,t+1) = q(k,t)*[P_0(k,t)+P_1(k,t)*r(k,t)]$$

$$+ (1-q(k,t))*[P_1(k,t)*(1-r(k,t))+P_2(k,t)r(k,t)]$$

$$1 \le k \le n \qquad (14)$$

$$P_m(k,t+1) = q(k,t)*[P_{m-1}(k,t)*(1-r(k,t))+P_m(k,t)*r(k,t)]$$

$$1 \leq k \leq n \qquad\qquad (15)$$

Similar to the single buffer case, $q(1,t)$ is the only known parameter in the beginning of the analysis. By using the following iteration procedures, the value of any desired variables can be computed:

(1) initialize all values to zeros except $P_0(all\ stages,0)$ and $q(0,1)$ are equal to 1,

(2) compute $P_j(all\ stages,t+1)$ according to $P_j(stage,t)$,

(3) compute $q(stage\ 1..n,t)$ according to $P_j(stage-1,t)$,

(4) compute $r(n,t)$ accord to $q(n,t)$ and $P_0(n-1,t)$,

(5) compute $r(stage\ 0..n-1,t)$ according to $q(stage+1,t)$ and $P_j(stage+1,t)$,

(6) repeat (2), (3), (4) and (5).

Because there is no closed-form solution for the above equations, the steady-state solutions required to find out the performance index are computed after a number of iterations until the outputs of these equations reach their steady-state, i.e. the differences between iterations are less than certain values. Details of this procedure will be discussed in section 4.5.5.

Once in the steady state, the probability that a packet arrives at an output port is defined as the normalized throughput S. That is

$$S = (1-P_0(n)) * r(n) \qquad\qquad (16)$$

Let $R(k)$ be the probability that a packet in a buffer of an SE in stage k is able to move forward. Then the normalized delay d can be given as

$$d = \frac{1}{n} * \sum_{k=1}^{n} \frac{1}{R(k)} \qquad\qquad (17)$$

where $R(k) = r(k) * \sum_{i=1}^{m} \frac{P_i(k)}{1 - P_0(k)} * \frac{1}{i}$.

4.4 The MIN Simulator

In order to verify the analytical model developed by Yoon et al., a simulator is built to analyze the errors and find out the impact and effect of the assumptions on the analytical model. Also, with the simulator, a platform is provided so that more realistic input patterns can be tested.

4.4.1 Simulator Design Principles

From the beginning of a clock cycle, the input to each input port is computed based on the average arrival rate m. Two random number generators are used to construct the packet arrival process. The first one determines whether there is a packet transmission request or not. If there is a packet generated, the second random number generator is used to determine the destining port address. Thus the arrival process is memoryless and the traffic is uniformly distributed all over the network.

For each cycle, all the switching elements in the system are examined. An SE at stage k will check the packet at the head of its buffer and route the packet according to its proper destination address. The routing in a delta network is controlled by the target address, i.e. the k_{th} digit of the destination address represents the local destination port in the k_{th} SE. An SE will first check the buffer in the destination SE at the $(k+1)_{th}$ stage. If a packet can be moved forward, the buffer management procedure is activated in both the two SEs. It is assumed that the destination port has a service rate of infinity. Thus a packet at the buffer of the $(n-2)_{th}$ stage SE is always able to move forward. The data which is required to compute normalized throughput is collect at the destination port of the final (i.e. the $(n-1)_{th}$ stage) SE.

This simulation program is developed in C language. Simulations with network size less than *1024x1024* nodes can be simulated in an MS-DOS environment while the simulation of larger networks can be performed in the UNIX environment (LINUX and SUN OS).

4.4.2 Limitations of the MIN Simulator

Some part of the MIN simulator can be improved further so that more realistic conditions can be simulated. They are as follows:

(1) Blocking packets: The current simulator follows the assumption that blocked packets will not issue further request in the next cycle. This is not true for most real-world cases. Details of this issue will be discussed in Section 4.5.

(2) Bias in contention resolution: When two or more packets are routed to the same destination port of an SE, the current simulator will choose the packet from the SE with smallest identification. Thus, SEs with smaller identification numbers have more advantages over SEs with larger identifications. Contention resolution can be further refined by using random logic or priority-based algorithms.

(3) Variable packet size: The packet size in the current simulator is fixed. In practical cases, packets may have different sizes.

(4) Limited buffer size of the first-stage SEs: In order to simulate more realistic networks, the buffer size of switching elements located in the first stage should be

much larger than that of the later stages. It is because the first-stage SEs are used to simulate real nodes that can normally hold more data and reissue requests for blocked packets for a long time period.

4.4.3 Simulation Results

The results from the simulations were shown to agree with the results from the analytical model with requisite input patterns. When the input patterns differ from the assumptions, the simulator shows results that can be explained with reasonable causes. The detailed results are shown in the Section 4.5.

In order to obtain the steady-state results, sufficient number of packets and clock cycles are needed. All the simulation results shown in Section 4.5 were obtained with a simulated running time of *500* clock cycles.

4.5 Results and Analysis
4.5.1 Input Load vs. Throughput and Delay

Two observations can be made from the results shown in Figure 4.5, 4.6, 4.7, and 4.8. First, increasing buffer size of SEs will benefit the overall throughput of the system. The throughput of the system is seen to increase linearly as the arrival rate increases (see Figure 4.5) until the system is saturated. The incremental throughput in the high arrival rate region is very small as the buffer size increases. This indicates that the improvement made by adding buffers will be very expensive when the average arrival rate is high.

Second, adding buffers will result in longer delay for packets to go through the network (shown in Figure 4.6). The delay increases as the arrival rate grows regardless

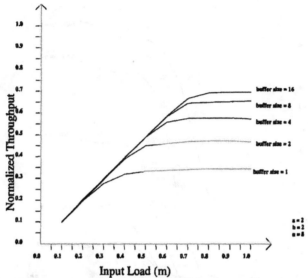

Figure 4.5 Normalized throughput of MINs with various buffer sizes and input rate.

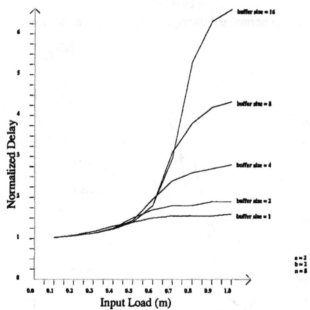

Figure 4.6 Normalized delay of MINs with various buffer sizes and input rate.

whether the network is saturated or not. We can conclude from the results that the normalized delay increases exponentially with respect to the input load.

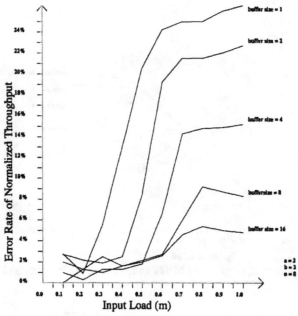

Figure 4.7 Error rate of normalized throughput with various buffer size and input rate.

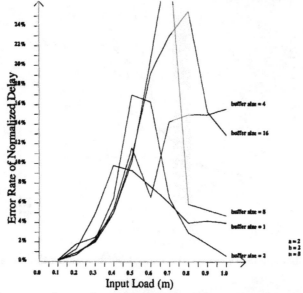

Figure 4.8 Error rate of normalized delay with various buffer size and input rate.

Comparing the analytical model of Yoon et al. and the simulation results, we can see that the analytical model has high errors for predicting normalized throughput (shown in Figure 4.7) when buffer size is small and input rate is high. Another observation from the results in Figure 4.8 is that the analytical model has larger errors in predicting delays when the average arrival rate is between 0.4 and 0.8. For the first case, with high input rate and small buffer size, there are many packets that are dropped by the switching elements because of network contentions (i.e. packets, that either cannot enter the network because of blocking in the first stage or are dropped by the intermediate nodes because their buffers are full, are not considered in the analytical model). For the second case, because the way the analytical model handles the network contention resolution and the distribution of destination addresses of packets are different from that of the real networks (as well as that of the simulator), the effect of buffering is more apparent in the middle input rate range than that of the two ends. In other words, when a packet is blocked in an intermediate node, in the analytical model, the packet will try again in the next cycle with the probability

$$m = 1 - (1 - \frac{m_{Previous\_Stage}}{b})^a,$$

where m is the input rate of an a-by-b switching elements in an MIN network, and with a new destination address determined by uniform distribution. On the other hand, in a real network, a blocked packet will try again in the next cycle with probably 1 and with the original destination address. When the input rate is small, there are few packets in the network and, consequently, the network contention is low. On the other hand, when the input rate is high, the network contention in the first few stages of the network is much

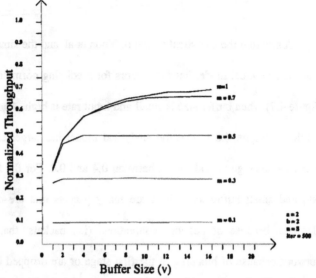

Figure 4.9 Normalized throughput of MINs with various buffer sizes under different input rate. Network size is $2^8 x 2^8$.

severe than that of the later stages. This results in that the network contention in the later stages of the network is not as intensive as that in the middle input rate range. Therefore, the error is lower in the two ends of the input load range than that of the middle range.

4.5.2 Buffer Size vs. Normalized Throughput and Delay

Figure 4.9 and 4.10 show that the normalized throughput increases with the buffer size, although it will become steady when the buffer size meets the demand from the average arrival rate and the constraints from network configurations. Figure 4.10 shows the effect of various buffer sizes on system throughput rate when the MIN network scales in size. The results indicate that the cost-to-performance ratio climbs rapidly as more buffers are added in SEs. Compared to throughput rate cases, normalized delay is more predictable under different buffer and network sizes. Figure 4.11 shows a constant linear property between the buffer size and normalized delays for different network sizes.

The assessments are as follows: First, if the average arrival rate is known in advance, the optimal buffer size (in the sense of cost-to-performance ratio) can be found by either the analytical model or the simulation results. Second, the number of stages in an MIN network has downward effects on the overall performance. This shows the fact that a crossbar network (an MIN network with only one stage) has the best performance over all other MIN networks.

4.5.3 Network Size vs. Normalized Throughput and Delay

As mentioned in Section 4.5.2, the throughput of an MIN is not linearly related to its network size. Figure 4.12 shows the impacts of changing network sizes on the normalized throughput rate. When the buffer size is small, the normalized throughput will decay quickly when the network scales its size. Figure 4.13 presents interesting results: The normalized delay decreases as the MIN network increases in size. For example, with mean arrival rate *1* and buffer size *16*, the normalized delay of an MIN network of size *2x2* is *16*. When the network size is scaled to *256x256*, the normalized delay decreases to *8*! The reasoning is that: for multiple stage networks, the queuing length of buffers at later stages is not as long as the queuing length in the first few stages because of contentions and blocking. Considering the above two cases, MINs with sufficient buffers show to be very cost-to-performance efficient for moderate network sizes.

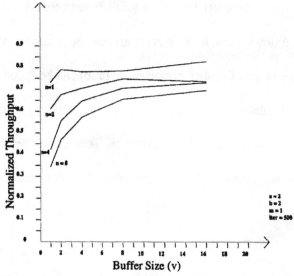

Figure 4.10 Normalized throughput of MINs with network size $2^n x 2^n$ and various buffer sizes.

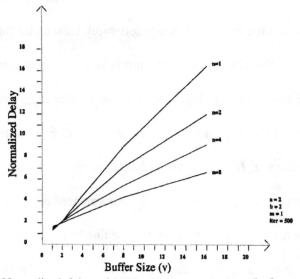

Figure 4.11 Normalized delay of MINs with network size $2^n x 2^n$ and various buffer sizes.

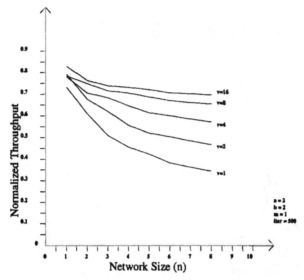

Figure 4.12 Normalized throughput of different MIN sizes for various buffer sizes.

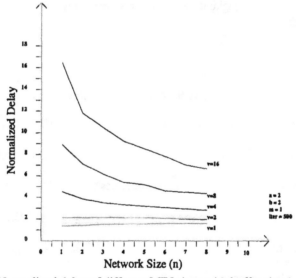

Figure 4.13 Normalized delay of different MIN sizes with buffer size 1, 2, 4, 8, and 16.

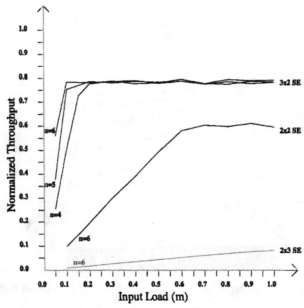

Figure 4.14 Normalized throughput versus various arrival rate for different types of switching elements.

4.5.4 Switch Element Types vs. Normalized Throughput and Delay

In this section, different types of switching elements are considered in constructing MINs. Compared to *2x2* SEs, the *3x2* SE networks have a nearly fixed normalized throughput (Figure 4.14) because the network becomes saturated even when the input load is very small (compared to *2x2* SE networks). For example, in a *243x32* (*a=3, b=2, n=5*) delta network, the network will become saturated when the average arrival rate is larger than *0.13*. The saturated point will become smaller when the network size increases. This type of network may only be suitable for networks that have a very small arrival rate. Contrast to the case of networks with *3x2* SEs, *2x3* SE networks have a

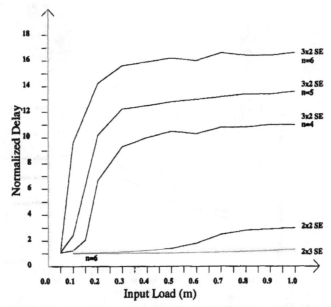

Figure 4.15 Normalized delay versus various arrival rate with different types of switching elements.

linearly increasing normalized throughput (i.e. no saturation point) since the network never saturates even when the input load equal to *1*.

The normalized delay of *3x2* SE networks is larger than *2x2* SE networks (shown in Figure 4.15) since packets have higher probability in losing in competitions with other packets. This results in longer queuing length in SEs. Conversely, the *2x3* SE network has a fixed normalized delay because packets are distributed sparsely in the network. In this case, packets rarely compete with other packets in SEs.

The errors between the analytic model and the simulation results are shown to be large in this section. As mentioned in the study by Yoon et al. [Yoon 1990], the equations are based on the uniform traffic assumptions. The traffic conditions discussed in this section are different from stage to stage. In addition, referring to Section 4.5.1 and note that the analytical model is prone to have a high error rate when the average arrival rate is

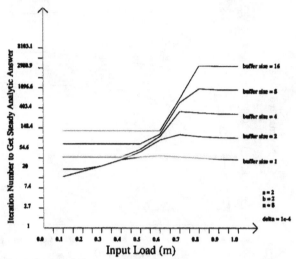

Figure 4.16 Number of iterations required to compute the analytical model results, i.e. the iterations needed to reach steady state, with various arrival rates. The network size is $2^8 x 2^8$.

high. The configurations that use $3x2$ SEs have very low saturated average arrival rate. This can be used to explain the larger error rate in this section.

4.5.5 Number of Iterations Needed to Compute Analytic Results

It is interesting to find out how many iterations are needed to compute the analytical results. As mentioned in Section 4.3, the number of iterations is the time needed for the network to reach its steady state when the input load is fixed. Figure 4.16 shows the iteration number versus various average arrival rates. The steady state case is defined as the differences between consecutive iterative computation of normalized throughput and delay is less than a threshold value δ (e.g. $\delta = 10^{-4}$ in this dissertation). The results show that the iteration number is a floor function with respect to the average arrival rate. When the input load is low, it needs a fixed number of iterations to compute the answer just like

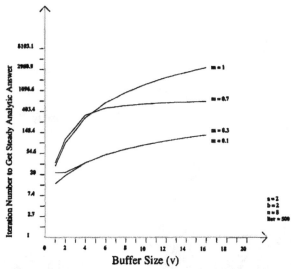

Figure 4.17 Number of iterations needed to compute analytical model results, i.e. to reach steady state, with various buffer sizes.

packets need a minimum number of steps to pass the network. On the other hand, when the input load is high, the network is nearly full, the iteration numbers will not increase after the saturation points that we found in Figure 4.6.

Figure 4.17 shows a plot of iteration numbers versus buffer size. The iteration number grows exponentially with respect to buffer sizes. This trend becomes more apparent when the input load is high. From the results gathered in previous sections, it is found that the behavior of MINs is predictable. An MIN system can be built to meet required specifications as long as the average arrival rate is known in advance. Our studies also show that the analytical model is capable of computing the performance index quite accurately compared to the simulation results. The advantage of using the analytical model is its short computation time. In the experiments, a simulation run of a $2^8 x 2^8$ MIN took minutes (depending on the buffer size and the arrival rate) to be

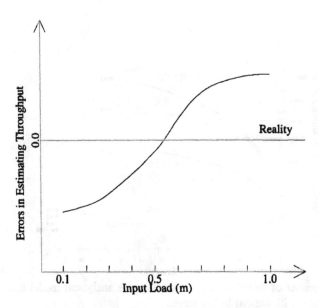

Figure 4.18 Trend of differences between the realistic MIN and the analytical model.

completed by an Intel 80486 personal computer while the results from the analytical model can be retrieved within seconds. Thus, the analytical model is very valuable in systems with dynamic configuration capabilities. That is, it can be used to evaluate network performance of our target computing system in a real-time fashion.

4.5.6 Discrepancy Errors Between the Analytical Model and Real Networks

Due to the memoryless assumption, packets, which lose the competition for entering the first SE stage, are discarded without any further actions. Realistically, when a request is blocked in the current clock cycle, it would re-issue a request in the next cycle with probability I (i.e. instead of the average request rate), and the destination address should be the same as that determined earlier. As a result, the accuracy of this model will perform as shown in Figure 4.18. When the average arrival rate m is small and conflicts occurred, the analytical model will use average input rate m instead of 1. That is, the analytical model tends to reduce the number of packets in the network. So, the predicted throughput rate from this model will be lower than that of the real case. On the other hand, when m is high, contentions that happen in the last cycle should continue for the next few cycles. In other words, if more than two packets want to go through the same port, the contention resolution logic can only admit one packet to pass each cycle and the request rate will remain as 1 in the next cycle. However, in the analytical model, it is assumed to generate a new request with random destination so that there are too many packets compared to that of the real-world case. In this case, the derived throughput rate from the model will to higher than that in reality.

4.6 Non-Uniform Communication Latency Interconnection Networks

A uniform communication latency interconnection network is a special case of non-uniform communication latency (NUCL) interconnection networks. Literally, in a NUCL network, the number of nodes or switching elements required in a communication between two nodes can vary. Nodes in a NUCL network generally have a fixed and, generally, smaller degree of connection which allows the system to be scaled easily.

Analysis of UCL networks in previous sections provides many basic and helpful performance indicators for the study of NUCL networks. Relation and interactions among the key components (e.g. network sizes, buffer sizes, network loads...etc.) in UCL networks can be applied to observe and analyze the characteristics of NUCL networks.

4.6.1 Comparisons between Uniform and Non-Uniform Communication Latency Networks

Uniform Communication Latency (UCL) interconnection networks are the most popular interconnection architecture for parallel processing systems. Observations from the above analysis clearly illustrate the advantages of UCL interconnection networks:

(1) Simplicity: UCL interconnection networks afford simplicity in software. Compilers, schedulers and operation systems built upon architectures with UCL networks can be simplified because of the symmetric topology and same bi-directional communication pattern.

(2) Steady throughput: Studies in Section 4.5.1 and 4.5.2 indicate that the steady-state throughput rate can be raised by adding more buffers in the switching elements. Also, studies in Section 4.5.5 found that the time needed to reach steady state is also predictable under the same conditions. These features ease users in predicting communications performance between nodes.

(3) Predictable delay: Observing from previous studies, it is found that the steady-state network delay increases linearly with buffer size (see Figure 4.11), and the delay reduces when the network size is increased (see Figure 13) with sufficient buffer size. These features provide network designers a way to estimate the network performances and a shorter delay can be expected when network size grows.

Unfortunately, the mechanism used in implementing UCL network is not scaleable. Full crossbars can provide nearly uniform communication latencies, but the $O(n^2)$ hardware cost makes it virtually unscalable. MINs, which circumvent the bandwidth problems of bus-based systems and high hardware requirements of full crossbars, provide bandwidth that scales with machine size. However, this increased bandwidth comes at a price: all communication latencies increase with the number of nodes in the system. Since scalability is very important for a distributed system, the Non-Uniform Communication Latency (NUCL) interconnection networks may be more suitable for building distributed systems.

The most important characteristic of NUCL interconnection networks is that the node degree (i.e. the number of links of a node) is fixed. This feature makes NUCL networks easier to scale in size. Latencies of NUCL networks may not be as good as that of UCL networks for the same network size. Nonetheless, when the size of networks grows, some nodes in NUCL networks have the advantage of remaining close to one another regardless of network size. Therefore, as machine size increases, applications running on UCL networks face increasing latencies for all communications. On the other hand, with NUCL architectures, if applications or the system controlling body can be designed so that communication patterns favor nearby nodes, the system should be able to improve its performance depending on how the average communication distance is reduced.

4.6.2 Key Issues in Non-Uniform Communication Latency Interconnection Network

From the discussion in the previous section, it is clear that the key for NUCL networks to out-perform UCL networks is to exploit various locality properties embedded in the system and applications. Communication locality can be divided into two domains: the first one is application locality that is presented in the organization of an application.

The second one is architecture locality that represents the capability of an operation system or architecture to exploit application locality.

Similar to studies in cache memory designs, application locality can be further divided into two categories: temporal locality which represents the effect of decreasing the communication frequency between application threads, and spatial locality which represents the effects of affinity in the communication pattern among application threads. Johnson [Johnson 1992] suggests the following three approaches to reduce communication latencies:

Avoid long latency operations

This approach exploits temporal locality in the applications. Numerous researches have been done in this area by exploiting compilation techniques in enhancing data reuses in applications. Both UCL and NUCL network architecture allow exploitation of temporal locality.

Reduce communication latency

This approach exploits spatial locality in the applications and focuses on minimizing communication distance. Applications can be designed to have good spatial locality to the extent that their inter-thread and resource-acquiring communication graphs have relative low bisection width and high diameter. While NUCL architectures can exploit spatial locality by placing communication requests on nearby nodes so that average communication distance can be minimized, UCL architecture is only able to exploit spatial locality when there are more resource servers or application threads than nodes (i.e. overlapping communications with executing other threads). It is evident that the governing body of the system needs to be designed cooperatively with this idea to improve the performance.

<u>Tolerate long latency operations</u>

This approach focuses on software paradigms and processor architectures that allow useful works to overlay long latency operations.

Studies [Agarwal 1991][Johnson 1992] have shown that, for NUCL networks, exploiting localities can reduce bandwidth requirements of applications and network contentions more effectively than improving the backbone network components (i.e. faster switching elements and communication channels). The study by Johnson [Johnson 1992] shows that the spatial localities embedded in applications have direct impacts on the network performance in NUCL systems. However, the study also shows that the effectiveness of gaining performance by exploiting spatial localities depends upon the level of which the communication distances can be reduced by the system. Thus, in the Osculant scheme, we mainly exploit the second approach by trying to shorten the communication distance of resource requisitions and by increasing the number of threads and servers. Additionally, we exploit the third approach in scheduling techniques that overlap the resource transmission task execution time. With these approaches, the NUCL network systems will have a good potential for improving their performance over the UCL network systems especially when the network size is large.

4.7 Conclusions

The studies of UCL and NUCL networks in this chapter suggest that, in order to improve the performance of a distributed computing system, which is mostly connected by an NUCL network, one has to cleverly arrange the network dispositions to achieve better performance. The analytical model and simulations of multiple stage interconnection networks indicate that

(1) Throughput increases as the buffer size increases and is limited by the configuration of the MINs.

(2) Delay increases linearly with the buffer size but decreases when the network size grows.

(3) The performance of UCL network is predictable when the average arrival rate and the network configuration are known in advance.

(4) The analytical model, which is computationally efficient, provides adequate accurate performance estimations when the MIN is not saturated and the buffer size is sufficient.

Thus, a multiple stage interconnection network with optimal cost-to-performance ratio can be built. Specifically, for the studied Osculant scheduling scheme, observations suggest that network traffic in distributed computing systems can be predicted controlled by arranging the buffer sizes and communication lengths whenever the job arrival rate is known or predictable.

The studies on non-uniform communication latency (NUCL) networks suggest that they offer certain features that lack in the UCL networks such as scalability and shorter communication latencies. However, in order to obtain these benefits, resources and applications in such distributed systems must be carefully arranged and designed to exploit the locality characteristics. For instance, applications have to be implemented so that communication distance between threads is shortened, and communication latencies can be overlapped by other useful works and tasks. More importantly, the scheduling and resource management scheme of the distributed system has to assign tasks and allocate resources so that network traffic is confined and minimized. The Osculant scheduling scheme studied in this paper will focus on this field.

CHAPTER 5
OSCULANT SCHEDULING MECHANISMS

In this chapter, the details of the Osculant scheduling scheme will be discussed. In the first part, jobpost distribution protocols will be presented. Various bidding strategies will be discussed in Section 5.2. In Section 5.3, experimental results are analyzed. Section 5.4 presents the resource management scheme used in Osculant. In Section 5.5, conclusions are presented.

5.1 Jobpost Distribution Protocol

Jobpost distribution protocols are designed to distribute small packets to participating nodes that contain job profiles, resource locations, and execution specifications. Major concerns in designing the protocol are topology independence and jobpost efficiency because:

(1) The Osculant scheduler is designed for a distributed, heterogeneous computing environment; and

(2) Jobpost efficiency directly affects the capability of the scheduler to probe, to search, and to gather information in the system.

Two parameters control and indicate the performance of jobposting: jobpost constraint and jobpost coverage. The former limits the distance how far jobposts can go and controls the jobpost/bidding delays, where the later determines the range which

53

jobposts reached in a system. It also represents the optimization that a job achieves in the system.

5.1.1 Multi-layer Jobpost Protocol

Flooding broadcasting forms the basis of our jobpost distribution protocol. This technique guarantees that all nodes that meet the defined distribution rules will receive jobposts even when there are failures in the system.

Flooding Broadcast with Hub Number Constraints

A node is either *susceptible* (nodes never hear the jobpost) or *infectious* (nodes know the jobpost). When a susceptible node receives a jobpost, it becomes infectious and decreases the hub number constraint by one. Then it relays the jobpost to its neighbors. When an infectious node receives a jobpost that has been seen before or the hub number constraint it received is zero, it does not react.

Multi-layer Jobpost Protocol (MJP)

Multi-layer Jobpost Protocol (MJP) contains three major components:

(1) a flooding broadcast is used to distribute jobposts in a single jobpost/bidding layer;

(2) a jobpost constraint, in the unit of communication hubs, limits the range of jobpost distributions in a jobpost/bidding layer; and

(3) in multi-layer jobpost/bidding, the winner of current layer repeats the MJP until a node wins in consecutive jobpost/bidding layers.

MJP satisfies the goals of topology-independent jobposting, balancing and regulating jobpost/bidding delay, controlling the level of optimization, and self-organizing in the Osculant scheme. An example is shown in Figure 5.1.

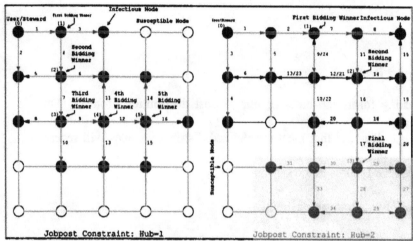

Figure 5.1 This figure shows an example of multi-layer jobpost/bidding. It indicates that *25* processors are connected by a mesh structure. With the jobpost constraint in the unit of hub number equals 1, as shown in the left figure, there are *5* levels of jobpost/bidding processes with a jobpost coverage of *60%* and with *16* messages. If the constraint is increased to *2*, it requires only *3* jobpost/bidding levels to have a jobpost coverage of *84% (21/25)*, and it needs to pass *34* messages.

Being an anomalous distribution protocol, MJP is convergent because, *infectious* nodes will neither re-post nor re-bid previous jobs. However, later studies remove this restraint (see Section 5.2). Convergence of MJP is then enforced by bidding strategies.

Balancing between jobpost/bidding overheads and level of optimization is an important issue in designing a distributed scheduler. A flat jobpost structure, that has loose job constraints, generally has higher jobpost coverage and, therefore, produces more optimal results. But this structure also is more vulnerable to high jobpost/bidding overheads because of failures in nodes or in communication channels. Moreover, there will be a greater message overhead burden (sending jobposts to *infectious* nodes). Conversely, distributions with restricted jobpost constraints normally have a quicker jobpost/bidding process, but have a more narrow scope in the system status. Consequently, such systems are inclined to become trapped at local optimums. Studies indicate that small jobpost constraints (*2* or *3* hubs) have sufficient jobpost coverage plus low overheads. Additional results can also be found in Section 5.3.

5.1.2 Other Jobpost Distribution Techniques

In some cases, such as in military applications, the number of messages traveled in the system must be minimized so that the probability of being detected or intercepted can be reduced. In a computing environment where customers will be charged for using communication channels, it is also desirable to reduce the number of messages in order to reduce cost. Therefore, by relaxing the requirement that all processors should receive jobposts in a jobpost/bidding layer, the number of messages transmitted in a system can be reduced. The candidates in this category contain epidemic algorithms and antientrophy algorithms [Chow 1996].

In most applications, it is not strictly required that all active processors receive jobposts and bid for jobs. Tasks can be completed as long as bidding participants can provide required system services. Therefore, the number of bidding participants only represents the level of optimization that can be obtained in the system. For example, in a distributed system with many resource suppliers, it is not necessary that all active agents join the jobpost/bidding process. Jobs still can be completed because resources are duplicated at many locations. The differences will be only cost and, possibly, service quality. Another distributed computing case is that: Accuracy of executing jobs can be guaranteed by setting appropriate read/write quorums to system functions. For example, by requiring all updated system functions or routines to be duplicated in more than half of the servers, it needs only half of the servers in the system to participate in the jobpost/bidding process to guarantee the correctness of processing.

5.1.3 Optimal Jobpost Distribution

The optimization criteria of jobpost distributions depend on the system configuration and job requirements. In this section, the criteria under investigation are message efficiency, jobpost coverage, and jobpost/bidding levels. The quality of a jobpost distribution method is determined by the ratio that it successfully reaches the best node, or the ratio of overall execution time from actual case to ideal case. In this section, the ideal case means a jobpost distribution with *100%* jobpost coverage and a uniform jobpost/bidding delay from any two processors in the system.

The example shown in Figure 5.1 displays the effect of jobpost constraints on jobpost distribution quality. In this section, the jobpost distribution is studied on a mesh structure. Jobposts are distributed by using the MJP with jobpost constraints in hub number. The bidding algorithm applied here is the performance-based bidding method (Details presented in Section 5.2.1). Jobs are generated with the same processing and I/O time, but with resources uniformly distributed in the system. Experimental results are summarized below:

<u>Jobpost coverage and message efficiency</u>

As shown in Figure 5.2a, the growth rate in the total number of messages is greater than that of the jobpost coverage with increasing hub number constraints. This means that, when the hub number increases, the number of redundant messages transmitted in the system increases in a faster rate. The MJP suppresses the number of nodes between

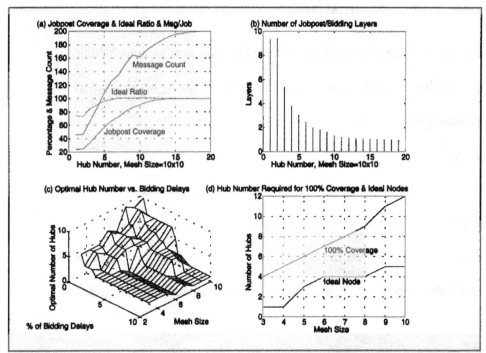

Figure 5.2 Simulation results and optimal jobpost constraints in hub number.

the new and old *stewards* in distributing old jobposts. However, this protocol cannot detect nodes that already knew the jobpost from previous broadcast processes. Therefore, in order to improve message efficiency, a less restricted jobpost protocol, e.g. epidemic algorithm, will be needed.

Number of jobpost/bidding layers

The number of jobpost/bidding layers decreases steadily as the hub number constraint increases (shown in Figure 5.2b). Job auction process in a *steward* is hold once all bids are received or once a pre-defined time-out period is reached. In general, a time-out period will be used only when there are failures in the system. So, in a system that is in its normal state, the auction delay is determined by the longest bidding delay between the *steward* and its child nodes. If the logical structure of an Osculant system is close to the under-lying physical structure, i.e. small hub numbers is equivalent to short bidding delays, more jobpost/bidding layers may have the advantage in achieving better message efficiency while providing sufficient jobpost coverage.

Resource distribution

For jobs with fixed resource servers, or for systems with large centralized resource servers, it is optimal to have small hub number constraints because the cost surface is mostly monotonically decreasing toward the optimal candidate node from any processor in the system. Small hub numbers will have highest message efficiency and the greatest scheduling quality.

Optimal jobpost constraints in hub number

The optimal hub number can be achieved in two ways. First, a system with long bidding delays will prefer to have small hub number constraints. This relation is shown in Figure 5.2c; the optimal hub number is generally a floor function of the bidding delays. For example, if the bidding delay is between *1%* to *4.5%* of the average job processing time, the optimal hub number constraint is *7* with the mesh size of *10x10*. If the bidding delay exceeds *5.5%*, the optimal value will drop to *1*. The second way is observed from the jobpost coverage and ideal ratios. Figure 5.2d indicates that the relation between the *100%* jobpost coverage and the *100%* ideal ratio is practically linear. Therefore, it is sufficient to achieve the optimal system performance by using a jobpost constraint that is about *75%* of the full jobpost coverage constraints. For instance, as shown in Figure 5.2d, in a *10x10* mesh, a hub number constraint of *5* is sufficient to reach the optimal system performance while the constraint for full jobpost coverage is *12*.

5.2 Bidding Strategies

Following Chapter 3, participating nodes submit bids that represent status, intention, or profit of nodes that can achieve from posting jobs. With additional considerations of the underlying computing environment, bidding processes are to be designed with the following purposes:

● Locally calculated bids: Participating nodes should calculate bids based on the information provided in the jobposts and local knowledge of the system status. The intention is to reduce the network traffic and to establish a loose, distributed and bottom-up scheduling style.

● Simple job auction process: The function of a *steward* node is to distribute jobposts, collect bids, and designate winning nodes in an Osculant system. Stewards should be kept as simple as possible. As a virtue of bottom-up and distributed system design, vital information must be kept locally. Therefore, the failure of a *steward* node, or any part in the system, will not represent a severe threat. In addition, the designed computing system can be easily reconfigured by choosing other nodes to serve as a *steward* at any moment.

5.2.1 Performance-based Bidding Method

The performance-based bidding method is the most basic bidding method. The objective is to balance loads of processing units and the network traffic connecting participating nodes. A good load-balanced system will generally have better performance because of reduced network congestion. With top-down scheduling schemes, load balancing can be achieved rather easily in a homogeneous and centralized computing system. Otherwise, load balancing is hard to achieve because of the difficulties in collecting local node status, and being aware of non-scheduled local events. In this method, bids are calculated locally by participating nodes to reflect the cost of completing jobs. Three key components of the performance-based bidding method are as follows:

Resource collection time estimation

An estimate of time elapse to collect resources distributed within a system is needed to define a rational bid. Prior to job execution, the required resources must be located, verified and possibly transmitted over the network. The resource transmission time is governed by the size of resources, cache storage status, local node I/O load, remote node I/O load, and network traffic. Of the five factors, the first three are known locally and can be correctly calculated. The other two factors must be estimated. Network bandwidth (or throughput rate) can be estimated by two ways. The first method sends a packet to probe the network status. It is obvious that this method will add to the network traffic. The other method is to estimate the traffic condition using indirect information. For example, the I/O load at remote nodes can be estimated by tracking previously received packets. Network traffic can be estimated in many ways. For instance, we can estimate the transmission time by counting the number of hubs between resource servers and bidders. The relationship between the bandwidth and distance can be defined using linear equations. This method will work as long as the network load is light. In this dissertation, we will use the network traffic model studied in Chapter 4 to estimate network bandwidth. Recalling that, in the UCL analytical model, network throughput rate can be found by giving the network configuration and average job I/O load information. The details of applying this model are presented in Appendix A.

Task execution time estimation

Local schedulers calculate the task execution time. For single-bidding strategies, a first-in-first-out (FIFO) scheduling scheme is employed. It is assumed that tasks are executed after all resources were received and previously assigned tasks were finished. Therefore,

$$Task\ Execution\ Time = Max(I/O\ time,\ Completion\ Time\ of\ Last\ Task)$$
$$+\ (Task\ CPU\ Time)$$

Bid suppression

Bid suppression methods play an important role in the Osculant scheduler design. Bid suppression is used to justify errors made in previously bidden jobs. Previous bidding errors are used to adjust bids applied to current jobs. Bid suppression can also be used to resist clustering of task assignments. Clustering occurs when tasks enter the system in blocks over a short time period because:

(1) nodes do not update their states (CPU, I/O and network load) until they receive job assignments; and

(2) there are time lapses among jobposting, bidding, and receiving task assignments.

Job assignments, therefore, for these tasks will be sent to the same node. The observed load diagrams for nodes without bid suppression generally have a "saw-tooth" shape. Short-term scheduling performance will be degraded. Thus, the design of bid suppressor contains two factors, namely the previous bidding errors and the number of jobs that are bided but not yet be assigned.

$$Suppressed\ Bid = Current\ Bid$$

$$* \ (1 + Bidding\_Error)^{MAX(Length\ of\ Job\ Queue,\ Number\ of\ Jobs\ Bided\ But\ Not\ Assigned)}$$

5.2.2 Energy-based Bidding Method

This method assumes that when information is transmitted between two nodes, two parties will be required to be active for the same time period. The overall energy consumed by the jobs is modeled to be:

$$Bid = (Task\ processing\ time) + (Estimated\ resource\ transmission\ time)*2$$

This is the simplest bidding algorithm in our studies. This method emphasizes the importance of network transmission time. Therefore, jobs with lowest transmission time will be favored by a bidding node. In other words, nodes that hold more resources will have advantages over other nodes.

5.2.3 Dynamic Jobpost Model

Jobposts are continuously updated or modified during the jobpost/bidding phase. Ideally, the information stored in the jobposts becomes more localized as they approach the final working node. In this model, bids calculated by the participating nodes will become more and more specific because the creditability of estimated system status is increased as the jobposts move closer to the future working-node. This model also provides resource forwarding capability. Resource forwarding scheme grants rights to intermediate nodes that keep valid copies of resources to distribute the resources to others. In this design, original resource servers will no longer supply all the file services to other nodes, but perform more "selective" tasks, like providing new resources to the system, managerial tasks, cache validations, and resource distribution management. The

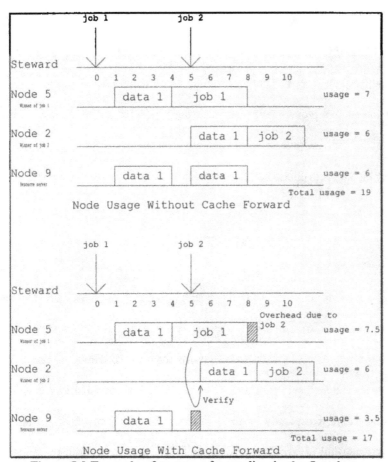

Figure 5.3 Example of resource forwarding in the Osculant.

work load and network traffic at resource nodes will, therefore, be reduced. Figure 5.3 illustrates the resource forwarding in the Osculant scheme.

The resource caching mechanism forms the basis of this bidding model. There are two bids that participating nodes need to concurrently calculate: the task-processing bid and the resource-supply bid. There are also two winners at each round of job auction process. The winner of the resource supply bidding updates the jobpost according to the local cache status and sends it to the task processing bidding winner. The next round of jobpost/bidding or job execution then can proceed. Resource verifications are performed before modifying the jobposts in order to ensure the correctness of jobposts.

The job auction process is the same as single-bid models. The winner of resource supply bidding and task processing bidding modifies the job profile. The winner of task processing bidding then distributes the new job profile to the next jobpost/bidding level.

5.2.4 Resource Contractor Bidding Model

Evolved from the dynamic jobpost model, there are also two bidding stages in this model. The winning node in the resource-supply bidding stage becomes the resource contractor that takes responsibility of collecting resources for jobs. Upon collecting all the required resources, the contractor node forwards them to the winner of task-processing bidding stage. The motivations of this model are that: first, the winning resource-supply nodes usually have, comparatively, more local resources and also have better channels (i.e. higher bandwidth) to access remote resources (e.g. gateway or bridge nodes). Second, we want to simplify the task of estimating network traffic among the bidders and resource holders by reducing the number of resource suppliers in the task-processing bidding stage. These arrangements will result in better bidding accuracy and local scheduling capability. This model also better suits the conventionally configured nodes in a local area network (LAN). In a LAN configuration, there are generally only a few nodes that can serve as local resource servers with better network and file service performance. In the resource contractor bidding model, these local servers autonomously become resource contractors and satisfy most local needs. Additionally, failures in local resource servers will only degrade system performance (i.e. resources will host remotely or migrate to less-capable nodes in the LAN), but will not halt services as in conventional systems. Furthermore, resource distribution management can be conveniently performed in the resource-supply bidding phase.

The resource contractor strategy is implemented by the two-stage bidding model plus a resource information exchange session. They are described as follows:

Resource-supply Bidding Stage

Participating nodes calculate bids that represent the cost of collecting all required resources. The single-bidding job auction model is applied in this stage. Winners at this stage become the *stewards* of second stage bidding. The final winners provide the following information in the jobposts that will be used in the second stage bidding:

(1) the identification of the resource-supplier node,

(2) the expected completion time to collect all resources, and

(3) the estimated I/O load after the completion of collecting resources.

Task-processing Bidding Stage

Participating nodes calculate the task processing bids by using information provided by the first stage winner. Because contractor nodes provide estimated resource waiting time, all required resources will be transmitted from only one node. Because the contractor node will, normally, locate locally, more accurate and aggressive local scheduling schemes can be applied. In the current implementation, task-processing bidding is held immediately after the assignment of resource contractor node. Bidders calculate their bids according to the current cache status (i.e. speculative estimation; no resource verification), network traffic between the contractor node and the bidder, and local CPU schedule.

<u>Cache Information Exchange</u>

In order to reduce communication overhead between the resource contractor and task-processing node, a resource information exchange session is performed right after the contractor node retrieves all resources from various servers. A packet with job resource list and current resource version number will be sent to the task process node in order to determine the types of resources to be transmitted.

<u>Out-of-order Local Scheduling (O3LS)</u>

O3LS becomes a feasible solution with the realization of two-stage bidding scheme. Contractor bidding model provides better-bounded information about the availability of future expected resources. Therefore, local nodes can make better estimates and utilize the system's resources more efficiently. O3LS is applied to local CPU time planning with non-preemptive scheduling techniques

5.3 Comparisons Among The Bidding Strategies

Experiments were conducted using the Osculant Simulator (see Section 3.2) with the job state diagram shown in Figure 3.3. The results shown in this session were obtained by using the configuration described in Appendix A. It should be noted that, in order to study the scheduling and resource management performance of the Osculant scheme, the spatial locality of applications are intentionally disrupted in the following simulations. That is, resources required by tasks were uniformed distributed in the simulated computing environment. The studied scheme will need to manipulate its scheduling and resource relocation policies to improve the system performance.

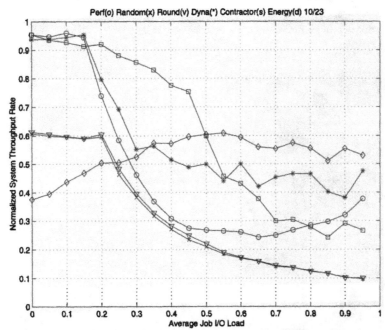

Figure 5.4 System throughput rate results of various bidding strategies.

5.3.1 System Throughput Rate

System throughput rate (shown in Figure 5.4) illustrates the capability of the scheduling scheme to utilize the system's resources. The results demonstrate different characteristics of these bidding models with respect to changing system configurations and job combinations. In general, multiple-bidding models outpace single-bidding methods, especially in a CPU-intensive computing environment. The performance-based method has the best throughput rate if average I/O load of tasks is below *10%*. Resource contractor model performs well over job I/O ratios ranging from *15%* to *50%*. The advantages of contractor bidding scheme gradually gives way to the dynamic jobpost method, or even the performance-based bidding method, as more I/O intensive jobs enter the system. Weak performance of contractor model in the low and high I/O load regions

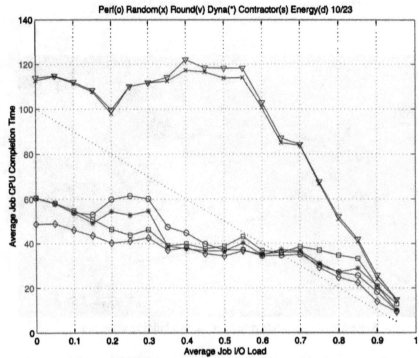

Figure 5.5 Average task CPU time consumption of various bidding strategies.

comes from excessive bidding stages and resource transmission sessions. In an environment where timing and task execution sequencing are enforced, the complexity of implementing contractor model will be of concern. When the average I/O load exceeds 50%, energy-based bidding method behaves surprisingly well. Tasks are found to be assigned mostly to nodes near resource servers. Depending on job composition, the overall performance of these bidding methods varies. Assuming distributions of job generation locations and compositions (in CPU time and I/O load) are uniform, system throughput rate improved by *54%, 95%, 102%* and *74%* over the random method for performance-based models, dynamic jobpost models, resource contractor models, and energy-based bidding models, respectively.

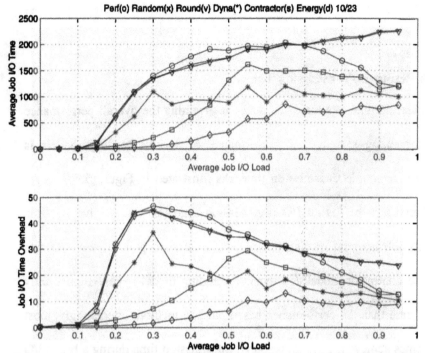

Figure 5.6 Average task resource transmission time of various bidding strategies.

5.3.2 Average CPU Time Consumption

The results in Figure 5.5 show the adaptability of bidding schemes. The sample jobs have mean CPU processing time ranging from *100* (no I/O) to *5* (*95% I/O time*) time units (shown in dotted line in Figure 5.5). The nodes, on the other hand, have a mean CPU processing power of unity. The bidding schemes are efficient in scheduling jobs to high power computing nodes. Furthermore, bidding schemes in Osculant are immune to performance degradation caused by system configuration alterations and by load fluctuations in top-down scheduling methods.

5.3.3 Average Job Resource Transmission Time

Task communication time is a major factor in determining the overall performance of a distributed computing system. The performance of various bidding models is strongly influenced by resource transmission time. As illustrated in Figure 5.6, energy-based bidding scheme has the lowest I/O transmission time (as well as the I/O time overhead), while its job assignment distribution performance is poor in low I/O rate region. The resource contractor model and dynamic bidding model have a significantly lower transmission time than the performance-based bidding method. Interestingly, most of the bidding schemes achieve a constant resource transmission time during a broad I/O ratio range. This is a result of low job completion rate and saturated network traffic. The lower graph in Figure 5.6 shows the transmission time overhead of completed jobs. This graph can be used to identify when the network saturates. For example, in the resource contractor model, the network saturation point is around *0.55*. After this point, the network will be fully loaded and, hence, the job completion time will be delayed. For jobs that can be completed by the simulation time deadline, however, their overheads are smaller then those of jobs with I/O load nears the saturate point. The reason is that there are fewer contentions in the network because most of them are queued at the resource servers. This provides an interesting analogue to the analytical model and simulator of multiple stage interconnection networks discussed in Chapter 4. In the middle I/O load range, the system status is difficult to estimate (i.e. the bids are less accurate). On the other hand, when I/O load is very low or very high, predictions of transmission time are usually close to the actual time.

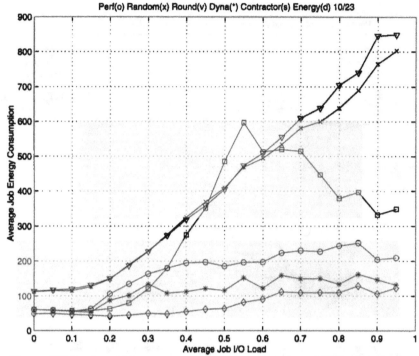

Figure 5.7 Average job energy consumption of various bidding strategies.

5.3.4 Average Job Energy Consumption

Energy consumption rate (shown in Figure 5.7) is defined as the time period that nodes need to be active because of assigned jobs. Overlaps in the communication time of newly assigned jobs and the processing time of previous jobs contribute to energy savings. Compared to system throughput rate, these results are very different among various bidding schemes. The contractor bidding method shows a relatively high average energy consumption rate because of its two resource transmission sessions. Overlaps in the resource contractor session are relatively small because the contractor rarely receives task-processing assignments. In contrast, the energy-based bidding model demonstrates the lowest energy consumption rate for almost all ranges. In summary, average job energy

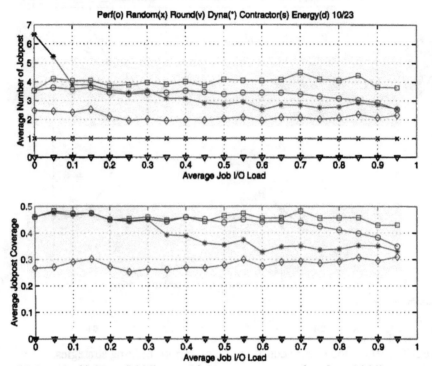

Figure 5.8 Level of jobpost/bidding and jobpost coverage of various bidding strategies.

consumption reduction from the bidding methods are significant. With the same job distribution in the throughput rate section, completed jobs utilize *42%*, *29%*, *73%* and *19%* of power consumed by jobs in the random method for the performance-based scheme, dynamic jobpost scheme, resource contractor scheme, and energy-based bidding scheme, respectively.

5.3.5 Average Jobpost Coverage and Jobpost/bidding Delay

As discussed in Section 5.1, jobpost constraints and the number of jobpost/bidding levels control the degree of optimizations that jobs can find in the system. This statement is argumentatively correct for single bidding schemes. The experimental results show that

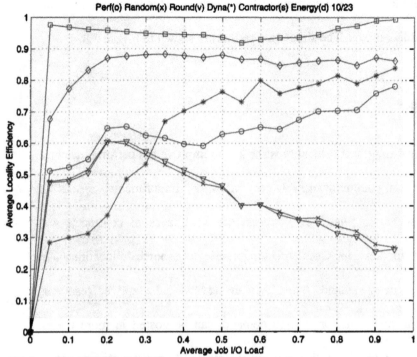

Figure 5.9 Locality efficiencies of various bidding strategies.

the resource contractor model has the highest jobpost coverage. The same model also has the greatest levels of jobpost-bidding because of the two-stage bidding. The dynamic jobpost model, which has moderate number in jobpost/bidding levels but a low jobpost coverage, suggests the effectiveness of dynamic jobpost modifications in finding more detail local information than other bidding methods. Unfortunately, dynamic jobpost modifications also increase the possibility of being trapped in a local optimal location. This correlation may explain the unsatisfied performance of this model in the mid-high job I/O load range. The energy-based bidding model has a surprisingly low number in jobpost/bidding levels, which results in low bidding delay, and moderate jobpost coverage. The results show that this model performs best in medium-high job I/O load range. In the I/O intensive environment, jobs are better assigned to resource servers (or to their neighboring nodes) to reduce the communication overhead. This is exactly the goal of the energy-based bidding model. The simulation results are shown in Figure 5.8.

5.3.6 Locality Efficiency

Studies in Chapter 4 suggest that locality is the key to improve the performance of a system with non-uniform communication latency network. Experimental results in locality efficiencies (shown in Figure 5.9) suggest the advantages of contractor and energy-based bidding models. In Osculant, the transient resource allocations are autonomous and are driven by demands. Thus, they are flexible and adaptive. Resources that are vital to system operations, or in high demand, can be hosted in more nodes. Otherwise, a minimum number of duplications are maintained to reserve storage space. Moreover, controlling the number of duplications improves the variety of replicated resources, which contributes to the reliability of the system.

5.4 Resource Management Schemes

The current implementation of the Osculant scheduler includes an integrated resource management scheme to improve the system performance. It is evident that proper resource allocations are essential to improve system performance. Network performance studies in Chapter 4 also conclude that the scheduling scheme should be able to exploit locality properties embedded in the network infrastructure and the jobs to further improve the system performance. Besides, while more copies of same resources improve the performance of some tasks, it is also desired to have more types of resources duplicated and distributed so that the designed system can be more robust and balanced.

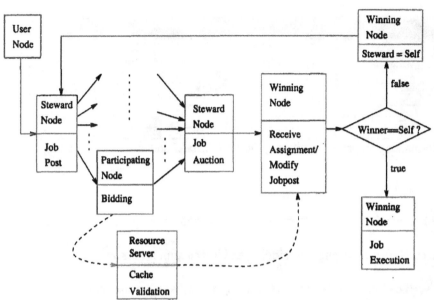

Figure 5.10 Resource validation process in the Osculant scheme.

In Osculant, the resource distribution scheme is implemented by various file caching and forwarding techniques. The resource management scheme is driven in a bottom-up manner and grants the responsibility of resource allocation, coherence maintenance, and distribution pattern enforcement.

Figure 5.10 shows the resource validation process in the Osculant scheduling scheme. Nodes will issue resource verification requests to resource servers upon receiving jobposts. In order to reduce the bidding delays, bids are calculated before knowing the verification results (i.e. speculative bidding). It is possible that a node receives job assignments based on expired cached copies. This type of error is treated as bidding errors and generally does not repeat itself in the next bidding because the assigned job will miss the predicted completion time. Bidding errors in this case do not affect the correctness of job executions because resource verification results are required

				ResCont1	ResCont2	Energy
Average CPU Time	-0.0882	-0.1886	-0.1863	-0.0234	-0.0144	-0.1705
Average I/O Time	-0.2000	-0.4273	-0.3843	-0.4655	-0.3202	-0.6296
Energy Consumption	-0.2033	-0.3971	-0.3933	-0.4681	-0.3496	-0.4309
Cache Hit Rate	2.8018	1.3488	1.5173	0.6177	0.8525	0.4181
Throughput Rate	0.3228	0.6848	0.6818	1.2414	0.8620	0.6377
I/O Ridding Error	-0.0734	-0.1207	-0.1413	-0.0968	-0.0454	-0.1180
Processing Time Error	-0.1502	0.8488	0.8320	-0.1863	-0.1200	-0.5517
Overall Utilization	0.0557	0.0365	0.0365	-0.2077	-0.1616	-0.3921
Server Utilization	-0.0610	-0.1007	-0.0927	-0.1738	-0.1247	-0.2660

Table 5.1 Performance comparisons between the *Plain Model* and *Request Frequency Model*.

prior to the job execution phase. Normally, resource validation process is completed earlier than the combined time length of bidding and job auction processes. By integrating the resource verification and bidding processes, there will be no extra overhead introduced in this resource management process.

Resource distribution control can be accomplished by the above resource management process, too. The number of duplicated resources can either be limited by the storage capacity of remote nodes or actively controlled by the resource servers. In the former case, the number and topology of duplications will be driven by the demands and system configurations. This model will improve the system performance but will also weaken the system reliability because some resources will not be replicated elsewhere. In the second case, we introduce active control mechanisms on the resource validation process so that more different types of resources can be replicated in the system. Two resource distribution models implemented in the Osculant are as follows:

Plain Model

This model is based on first-in-first-out (FIFO) principle. When a new node holds a copy of the resource, the oldest node in the list is flushed. From the experiments, it is shown this method is simple and introduces little network traffic for resource validation message exchanges. However, the trashing effect affects the overall performance because useful resources might be replaced or flushed by any newly requested resources.

Request Frequency Model

In this model, updates of resource entries are based on the frequency of validation requests. Resource servers maintain several counters that record the number of validation request from other nodes. The counter also decreases periodically according to the local clock. Simulation results indicate that this method is more efficient in reducing network traffic among nodes. Experimental results are shown in Table 5.1. However, this model cannot control the geology distribution of resources.

In the Osculant scheme, a node that updates its locally stored resources is required to notify the original resource servers about the changes. Consistency of duplicated resources will then be enforced since all nodes have to verify the correctness of their cached resources prior to the task execution phase. In case that there are more than one resource servers, the notified resource server has to propagate the updates to other resource servers using various commit protocols [Chow 1996]. However, update propagation in the Osculant should be kept in the level among the resources servers. Although it is possible to update all the replicated resources in the system, the cost of extra network traffic may be too high. Furthermore, most nodes in the Osculant are only caching the resource to reduce the resource transmission cost instead of intending to become replica servers. This means that the cached resources in nodes can be replaced very frequently.

5.5 Conclusions

In this chapter, we explore the scheduling techniques based the findings from previous chapters. Many interesting results, as well as many potential problems, were uncovered from these studies. For the jobpost distribution protocols, the multi-layer jobpost protocol (MJP) was established and studied to distribute jobpost to the system in a best-effort approach. Though it is clear that jobpost coverage rate is proportional to the optimal scheduling performance in a distributed system, the jobpost and bidding delays will nevertheless grow to an unbearable level when the system is large. Moreover, announcing jobs in a flat structure (for example, a system with only one *steward*) will make the system more vulnerable to system faults. Experiments show that MJP is capable of controlling the depth and width of each jobpost/bidding process. The results also show that small jobpost constraints are sufficient to distribute jobposts to the system with acceptable performance.

Since bidding strategies are at the heart of the Osculant scheduling scheme, we developed and tested several different approaches in this chapter. Listing in the order of increasing complexity and aggressiveness: they were, first, the *performance-based method*. Here, bidding nodes calculate their bids based on the job completion time. It is found that this method performs well in a lightly loaded system but performs badly in a heavy load system. It is clear that, without knowing the global system status, this method is not capable of delivering good scheduling performance in certain conditions. Next, in the *energy-based method*, we change the bidding components to the active time of nodes. Compared to the *performance-based method*, this method performed very well in heavy load systems because nodes want to conserve their active time and emphasize their network traffic load in their bid.

By realizing that single-bid methods did not perform well, we consider exploiting the locality principle discussed in Chapter 4. The first step is to build a mechanism so that local load information can be learned without broadcasting or polling processes. The *Dynamic Jobpost Model* applied this principle by granting the intermediate-level *stewards* the right to modify jobposts according to local information. With this arrangement, the accuracy of jobposts and bids can be improved. Experimental results show that the system throughput was increased by *27%* over the *performance-based method*.

In the *Resource Contractor Bidding Model*, we take further steps in exploiting the locality principle: First, we used the *dynamic jobpost model* to collect local information in the system. Then, by observing that resources are generally located in some "super" nodes in a distributed system, we split the bidding process into two phases. In the *Resource-supple bidding* phase, the scheduling scheme will designate a node to act as the *resource contractor* that is responsible for collecting and supplying all required resources. Next, the *resource contractor* initiates the *task-processing bidding* phase that finds the real working nodes. With this model, we can further improve the system throughput performance by *32%* over the *performance-based method*.

Following the discussions in Chapter 2, another technique to improve the network performance is to move servers and clients so that they can close to each other. Task scheduling is the typical way of relocating clients. In this chapter, we also exploit the technique ·of relocating resources (and even servers) in the system to reduce network traffic. Resources in Osculant scheduling scheme can be relocated to other nodes based on demands. This means resources can be duplicated and reused in nearby nodes. However, with the resource relocating, the coherence of resources must be maintained to guarantee the correctness of job processing. Hence, more network traffic will be introduced. Furthermore, it will be very difficult to define an analytical network traffic model with the resource relocating technique. In terms, it means that network communication delay will be more difficult to predict.

CHAPTER 6
DEVELOPMENT OF OSCULANT SHELL

Osculant scheduling studies were conducted by simulations, and implemented using a custom UNIX Osculant Shell. The Shell connects, monitors, bids, and distributes MATLAB jobs and executable objects among a collection of Hewlett Packard and SUN workstations. The studies also utilized a custom Osculant Job Profile Generator implemented in MATLAB script and C language. These two software systems define the Osculant experimental environment.

6.1 Structure and Implementation of Osculant Shell

Figure 6.1 shows the structure of Osculant Shell. The Osculant Shell consists of a collection of modules interconnected by various communication channels. Modules independently process information that runs simultaneously in the background. The shell is implemented in C language and Berkeley Sockets. The design of the Osculant environment is based on the consideration of portability and compatibility among other UNIX systems. The functions of modules are described in the following sections.

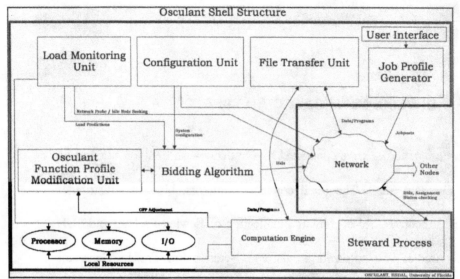

Fig 6.1 Structure of Osculant Structure.

6.2 Osculant Job Profile Generator

The basic market-driven philosophy underlying Osculant is one of competitive bidding. The key to successful bidding is to estimate accurately and efficiently the cost-complexity of a posted job. This is the role of the Job Profile Generator (JPG). Job profiles must be generated first from the information provided by the tasks that are distributed among participating nodes. Upon receiving the job profiles, distributed heterogeneous nodes calculate the completion cost of a task based on their interests, ethos, biases, and capabilities. The job will be assigned to the node by the *steward* with the best bid. The quality of JPG directly affects the bid accuracy and scheduling performance.

6.2.1 Design Principle and Algorithms

The JPG is responsible for creating job profiles that act as a unidirectional bridge between tasks and announcing their presence to the distributed heterogeneous computing system. Job profiles of announced tasks will be made available to the system prior to the job execution phase. In the case of Osculant, profiles are created prior to the bidding phase. The JPG uses source code or batch files of jobs to extract job profiles that contains

(1) information that can be used to estimate work loads of jobs,

(2) architecture specifications that are required to complete the jobs, and

(3) constraints needed to complete the assigned jobs.

Though profiling techniques, which are used to extract timing characteristics of computer programs, have been extensively studied and developed, relatively few studies have been done with the goal and approach described above. Park [Park 1989, 1993] and Shaw [Shaw 1989] developed a technique to predict deterministic timing behavior of programming in high-level languages with analytical models in evaluating the lower and upper bounds in program execution time. In the JPG, we concentrate our effort in extracting function statistics, which includes the frequency and granularity of function calls in a job, and resource requirements (instead of timing characteristics in previous studies) from the jobs because they can be better utilized in the target computing environment. That is, since the configuration and status of nodes can vary dramatically in a heterogeneous computing system, the information stored in job profiles should allow nodes to estimate the job completion cost according to their setup and status.

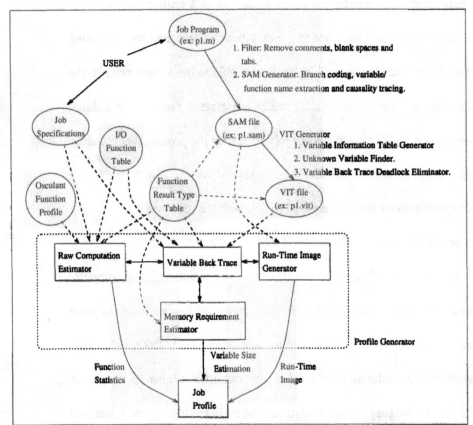

Figure 6.2 Structure of the Job Profile Generator. The filter process separates operands and operators. The SAM Generator process performs branch coding, variable extraction, and function name extraction. The Variable Information Table (VIT), which is a cross-reference table between the variables and functions, is generated by the VIT Generator. In the Job Profile Generator, the Variable Back Tracing engine estimates the value of and the size of variables.

Several support mechanisms were studied and built in the Osculant scheduler so that participating nodes can utilize them to construct job profiles and calculate the cost of job completion during bidding. The JPG support mechanisms are described as follows:

Function Result Type Tables (FRTT)

FRTT stores information regarding system functions. In some cases, FRTT entries are functions that have been previously profiled. Functions listed in the FRTT will be processed faster than from their source code once they are properly characterized. The FRTT can be modified during run-time to improve the estimation accuracy and execution efficiency. FRTT contains two libraries: (1) the Function Result Size Table (FRST), which is used to estimate variable sizes (for matrix) and values (for scalar variables), and (2) Osculant Function Profile (OFP), which is used to estimate function execution time. An example is provided in Appendix B.

Granularity Index

It is found that the computation loads for many classes of functions are not linear with respect to the size of input variables. The estimation of the computation load at the bidding nodes will, in these cases, need to be synthesized with some care. A possible solution is to implement a multi-mode, or high resolution Osculant Function Profiler (OFP) based on statistics of input variables for all function calls. It is impractical to send detailed variable size information in the job profiles since this would consume too much network bandwidth. For the designed JPG, the simplest measure of granularity was used where the granularity is represented by a number (i.e. granularity index) of an individual call. The results obtained to date are promising with small approximation errors.

Other Supporting Mechanisms

Several supporting mechanisms have been implemented to improve estimation accuracy and execution efficiency. For example: the *Location Information Adjustment* (LIA) procedure uses normalized weighted sum according to the proximity to the target variable to determine the results of variables. The *Variable Dimension Adjustment* procedure is used to utilize the information extracted by the pre-filtering process and modifies (reduces, in most cases) regarding variable size. The *Inline Scalar Evaluation* procedure evaluates values of scalar variables. And a JPG caching technique is developed to accelerate the job profile generation process. Detailed information of these procedures can be found in the study by Wu and Taylor [Wu 1997].

The heart of the profile generator is the *Variable Back Tracing* (VBT) engine. The VBT recursively traces the variables referenced by the target variable. The stop conditions of recursions are input parameters and explicitly defined variables in the program. The *Function Result Type Tables*, *Location Information Adjustment*, and *Inline Scalar Evaluation* procedures work cooperatively to find the final estimate of a target variable. The next step is to categorize the functions such that they can be traced properly. The first stage of classification determines the types of functions based the information stored in FRTT. Functions that are not in the FRTT will be considered as customer functions. The second stage of classification names types of operators and traces input parameters. Memory occupancies of tasks are determined at this stage. The structure of JPG is shown in Figure 6.2.

Figure 6.3 shows an example of the job profile for a test sample. Most of the job profiles are sparse and in integer format. Therefore, they can be compressed and efficiently transmitted. The resulting job profile not only provides essential information of tasks but also is easily computable. The current version of the Osculant Profile Generator is implemented in C language and MATLAB 4.0.

Experiments show that the error rate varies with respect to the actual computation load. The normalized error rate, which is found by normalizing errors with respect to real computation load of jobs, gives a better indication for the overall quality of the Osculant JPG. The normalized error rate for estimated computation load, which is the computation

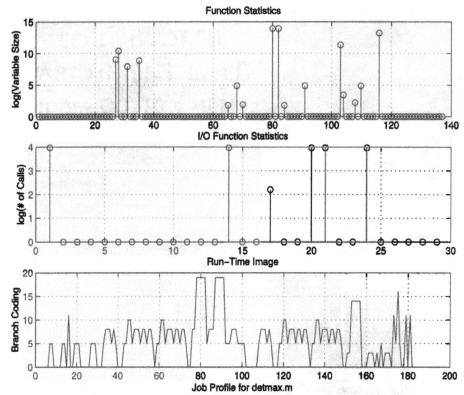

Figure 6.3 Example of job profile from the Osculant Job Profile Generator.

load estimated by the Osculant JPG, is 10.78%, and bidding estimates, which is the computation load estimated by bidding nodes, is 45.46%. When it was recorded, these estimations are made without actually executing the programs. The error rates are considered acceptable for the purpose of preliminary or first-time bidding.

6.2.2 Osculant Job Profile Retrospective

In an Osculant system, generating job profiles is the first step in the execution of a job. Typically, inaccurate job profiles normally will neither seriously degrade the overall system performance, nor produce incorrect results. Inaccuracy can be corrected or compensated for possibly in latter stages of job processing. For example, the bidding

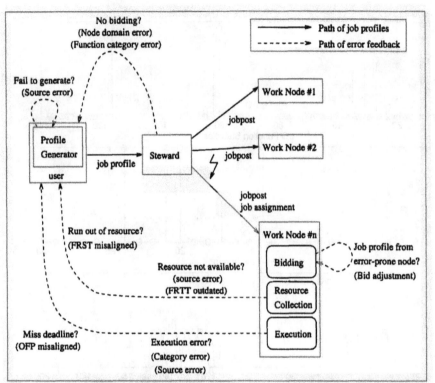

Figure 6.4 This figure shows the Osculant Job Profile Generator in the Osculant scheme. The accuracy and quality of job profiles can be fed back to the origin of the job profile from different stages of job executions.

process itself can correct the errors in job profiles. Furthermore, Osculant scheme contains close-loop feedback that can correct errors as well. Figure 6.4 shows the life cycle of jobs in the Osculant scheme based on the viewpoint of job profiles. Function category faults in generating profiles, for example, results in job rejections before job executions. Function profile inaccuracy results in degraded performance. These concerns can be easily corrected by adjusting the FRTT. A very sophisticated profile generator design, however, may not be worth the tradeoff for a decrease in generality and efficiency.

6.3 File Transfer Unit

The File Transfer Unit (FTU) transfers data among nodes. In Osculant, data and job files can be distributed within several nodes and transmissions can occur at any time. Performing multiple file transmission sessions will improve the performance of and the efficiency of communications. The FTU generates an individual process for each file transmission session.

File transmissions can be either active or passive, depending on what initiates the file transmission. In the active file transmission mode, the assigned node sets up the communication channels to the resource (e.g. data and job files) holders and "retrieves" the required data. This model is simple and fast, but is considered impractical and insecure. On the other hand, in the passive mode, a node receives a job assignment, and sends the request to resource holders, and then the resource holder initiates the transmission. Data is then "sent" to the assigned node. The passive model requires one extra message passing stage but is more secure and practical than the first method because the resource holders are mostly the file servers of a system.

To operate the Osculant Scheduler correctly and effectively, messages and data must be handled in a proper order. An FTU module has two message receiving and two message transmission queues. One pair of receiving/transmission queues, which use first-in-first-out policy, is dedicated to the transmission of data and job files. The other message queues are priority queues. The priorities of messages are:

(1) Status Request (highest priority)

(2) Status Reply

(3) Job Completion

(4) Job Deletion

(5) Job Assignment Acknowledgement

(6) Job Assignment

(7) Bid

(8) Jobpost

(9) User Input (lowest priority)

6.4 Steward Process

In Osculant, the *steward* performs the following functions: job auction, status checking, fault handling and node training. Because processors perform their bidding autonomously, and the *steward* has the full authority to award job assignments to any working node based on bids, some top-down capabilities can be implemented in the Osculant scheduler to achieve certain goals like fast job assignments or improving the overall scheduling performance.

Job auction processes are discussed in Chapter 5. The *steward* also performs status checking for the system. Normally, the *steward* has responsibility to check the status of its child nodes. Faults are handled by redoing jobpost/bidding process among active neighboring processors. The Osculant scheduler also provides top-down control over the system in training and monitoring of working nodes. The *steward* can log and evaluate the bidding performance of its child nodes. Top-down training can be accomplished by duplicating job assignments and sending them to both the node with best bid and the nodes that need further training. Therefore, training nodes can have more chances to calibrate their bidding components.

An additional feature of *steward* is its ability to perform reliable job processing. To perform reliable computing for an unreliable distributed system, a *steward* node can duplicate job assignments and send them to working nodes without sharing resources. Failures caused by crackdowns in any single resources, therefore, can be greatly reduced. Compared to other fault tolerance schemes, this method is the simplest to implement. This method also provides higher guarantee level in processing critical tasks in a real-time system.

6.5 Other Modules

The following modules are planned or partial implemented in the current version of Osculant Shell.

Configuration Unit

Configuration Unit (CU) dynamically changes the system configuration based on the system status or user demands. It also provides a transparent view of the system to the user. Main functions of CU contain:

- Connect/disconnect nodes: Disconnect failed nodes in order to reduce bidding delays and to re-connect recovered nodes to the system.

- Add/delete nodes: Accept new nodes to the system or delete nodes from participating list.

- Calibrate system parameters.

Load Monitoring Unit

The Load Monitoring Unit (LMU) provides local node information for the purpose of bid generation. LMU adjusts the local node performance parameters to adapt to the local load requirements set by the local owners as if these nodes are privately owned. The main functions of this LMU are:

- Modified "Ping" function, which probes the network status.

- Idle node hunter that estimates the computation resource of a subsystem.

- Algorithmtic estimates of communication channel bandwidth and throughput stability.

Osculant Function Profile Modification Unit

As described in Section 6.2, the Osculant Function Profile (OFP) stores information about system functions and provides the basis for calculating bids. The module modifies the contents of OFP in order to improve the bidding accuracy after completing all assigned jobs.

Computation Engine

The computation engine of current version of Osculant Shell is MATLAB. The cooperation of Osculant Shell and MATLAB is established by using MATLAB External Interfaces [MATLAB 1993]. The External Interface Library is MATLAB's application programming interface (API) and is called from the C language within the Osculant Shell. The interface routines will create two pipes so that data and commands are transmitted

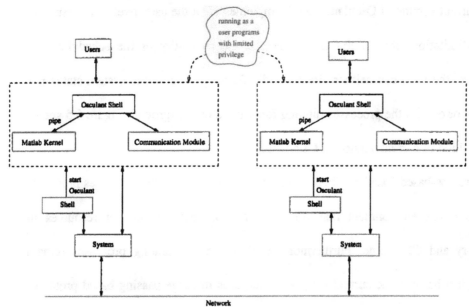

Figure 6.5 Location of the current version of Osculant Shell.

and executed by the MATLAB engine. The MATLAB External Interface Library provides a platform for heterogeneous computing environment while running on SUN, HP, and other systems. The current version of Osculant Shell also accepts executable binary objects to be scheduled and executed by the system. These jobs can, however, only be executed in homogeneous systems.

6.6 Future Developments

The current version of the Osculant Shell is used for evaluation and demonstration purposes. The scheduling overhead is too high for serious applications. To move Osculant Shell to the next level, some key developments and improvements are needed. They are described below:

- The current version of Osculant Shell is implemented at the user level. This results in many limitations that inhibit the scope and the capability of the scheduler. For instance, the shell can neither directly and efficiently observe the system status nor change or control the processes running foreground or background. Figure 6.5 shows the position of current version of Osculant Shell.

- The process-based Osculant Shell is currently inefficient because it creates processes in the UNIX environment that consumes a substantial amount of resources in memory and CPU time. Furthermore, communications among processes remain inefficient because the current Osculant Shell uses message passing based protocols and mechanisms. It is better for the Osculant Shell to be implemented by thread-based structure.

The repositioning of the Osculant Shell in an operation system requires additional planning. As mentioned above, the shell should be located in a lower level of a system to improve the performance. However, implementing the Osculant Shell in a very low level reduces the possibility of porting it to other heterogeneous systems. To implement the Osculant Shell in a way that balances the need for performance and for portability, a good location for the Osculant Shell is between the command shell and the system kernel.

CHAPTER 7
CONCLUSIONS

In this chapter we review the contribution of this dissertation, and allude to the possible extensions and future research for the work presented.

7.1 Research Contributions

In this dissertation, a new scheduling scheme, called Osculant, is studied. The Osculant scheduler is bottom-up, self-regulated, and designed for distributed heterogeneous computing systems.

Performance evaluations of uniform latency communication (UCL) and non-uniform latency communication (NUCL) networks were performed in Chapter 4. By studying the analytical model and simulation results of UCL networks, we found that network performance can be predictable if the job arrival rate is known in advance. Also, in a system with UCL network configuration, a system with optimal performance-to-cost ratio can be built. These two properties of UCL networks make the scheduling simpler and yield better overall performance. However, UCL networks are difficult to scale in size. The $O(n^2)$ cost growth rate of crossbar networks ($O(n*log(n)$ for delta networks) with respect to system size prohibits it to be applied in general distributed computing systems. Conversely, NUCL networks are more scalable and economical in cost but are also more difficult to predict the communication performance. To cope with the possible performance degrades from NUCL networks, application locality and architecture locality have to be enforced to reduce the network traffic. Localities of applications and resources can be handily manipulated by the Osculant scheduling scheme.

Several new dynamic bidding strategies were introduced and investigated. Compared to the random scheduling scheme, the *performance-bidding method* improves load balance and allows a *54%* higher system throughput rate. The *energy-based bidding method*, which focuses on low job completion cost, can reduce the average job energy consumption rate by *80%*. Multiple-bid methods were designed to correct the shortcomings of single-bid strategies (e.g., the *performance-* and *energy-based bidding methods*) and improve bidding accuracy and system performance. *Dynamic Jobpost Bidding Model* and *Resource Contractor Bidding Model* are two examples of this category. Experiments show very promising performance growth over the single-bid methods. With experiments in applying different bidding strategies, the system behavior is shown to be "turnable". That is, system ethos can be altered to suit for user demands and environmental changes by choosing different bidding methods. Moreover, with multiple-bid methods, system status information is progressively gathered through multiple job announcement and bidding steps. It is shown that scheduling overheads can be effectively reduced by this scheme.

Studies using the Osculant Shell provide simulated real-world experiences in implementing a distributed system. The Osculant Job Profile Generator (JPG) generates job profiles on-line such that other nodes can estimate the resource requirements and job completion cost. The experiments show that the quality of job profiles from JPG is adequate for preliminary bidding. The Multi-layer Jobpost Protocol (MJP) is developed to announce jobs to the computing system. The MJP is robust and self-regulated. The design of MJP also achieves the balance between improving job announcement coverage and reducing scheduling overheads. Studies of other modules in the Osculant Shell reveals even more potential of the Osculant scheduling scheme.

7.2 Limitations

Flexibility and versatility of the Osculant scheme, however, bring some negative effects to certain types of applications. For example, the multilayer jobpost/bidding structure makes the prediction of scheduling delay difficult especially when there are faulty nodes in the system. This means that the current Osculant scheme is not very suitable for real-time applications. One way to solve this problem is to use smaller bidding timeout and more restricted jobpost constraints. Nonetheless, these arrangements will hurt scheduling performance. Another concern of our scheme comes from the security issues. In order to make our scheme more flexible and scalable, a *steward* node does not maintain a list of its neighboring participant nodes. This approach enables our scheduling scheme to spawn, grow, or reduce its system size according to the system status. Notwithstanding, membership control becomes a problem with this design. How do we filter out jobs from outside nodes? Or how does a steward node distinguish bids from these unknown nodes and evaluate the credibility of their bids? One possible solution for the membership problem is to use various distributed commit protocols [Chow 1996] so that nodes in the system will know the existence of new members. Needless to say, this solution will increase network traffic and the workload of nodes.

7.3 Future Directions

In a computing system, resources are mostly requested in the high level format, e.g., system services comprised several low-level resources. In general, end-users or system processes have simple and abstract "goals" with regards how they schedule their jobs. Scheduling in the context of these "simple" goals is straightforward, but not likely to be optimal in performance. Furthermore, trends change in the future infrastructure of computing environment (e.g., modulated software applications, execution while downloading), task scheduling and resource management should evolve themselves with considerations of these ideas.

Motivations for such studies are based on the observation that task execution constraints can be refined, determined or even defined on the scheduling (or execution) time. As found in the Osculant studies, it is possible that a systematic and autonomous scheduling scheme can be developed so that the task completion cost can be minimized.

In terms of decision-making and service quality, timely completion, up-to-date information and confidence in estimating job completion cost play the key roles. The backbone scheduling scheme should be capable of operating in several modes simultaneously. The Osculant scheme has been shown to be flexible and versatile in performing multiple mode scheduling. Jobpost constraints, bidding strategies, and resource management methods can be tailed to accommodate system status and job specifications. In the wake of the development of task organizer technologies, the refinement of task specifications can further improve the system and cost efficiencies.

Furthermore, Osculant has been designed for an on-line scheduling system. Preferably, tasks can be scheduled and executed continually or with a constant waiting time. Thus, a *task organizer* with progressive output will be ideal. Among many optimization methods, a good candidate is simulated annealing (SA) [Rutenbar 1989]. Simulated annealing method accepts inputs with great temporal and spatial flexibility without seriously affecting results. Results form the simulated annealing can be retrievable at any moment because of its progressive processing nature. It also means that the organizer waiting time, which is controlled by the cooling schedule in SA, can be used as a control variable in determining the desired level of optimization for the current set of jobs.

Another possible research direction is the study of fault-tolerant capability of the Osculant scheme. It has been shown that, with the bottom-up approach, the Osculant scheme can survive many types of system failures. However, a better fault recovery scheme, for example, how to recover an assigned job if nodes or network were broken, still needs to be found. A simplest way to recover a failed job assignment is to wait for timeout and then re-post and bid the job. Obviously, this method is very inefficient when the level of post/bidding is high. As for the fault tolerant capability, the steward process discussed in Chapter 6 might be a good position to handle this type of problems.

APPENDIX A
SIMULATION CONFIGURATION

In Section 5.2, the simulation results reported were obtained from the Osculant Simulator with the following configurations.

A.1 Node Configuration

In this experiment, there are 49 nodes connected in a mesh topology. The node processing power is determined randomly using normal distribution with both mean and standard deviation equal to 1. Each node has a maximum communication bandwidth 1 to its neighbors. During bidding process, a node estimates the communication bandwidth to other nodes using the analytical network performance model discussed in Chapter 4. In calculating the estimated bandwidth, we used a multiple stage interconnection network configured with 2x2 switching elements, buffer size of 4, and a steady-state threshold of 0.001. The estimated throughput rate is shown in Figure A.1. The actual bandwidth between two nodes is affected by network traffic condition that will be discussed later in this section. All nodes have cache storage with the size of 10 units. Also, resource servers maintain resource validation tables for all resources that they host. The resource validation table records up to 10 different locations.

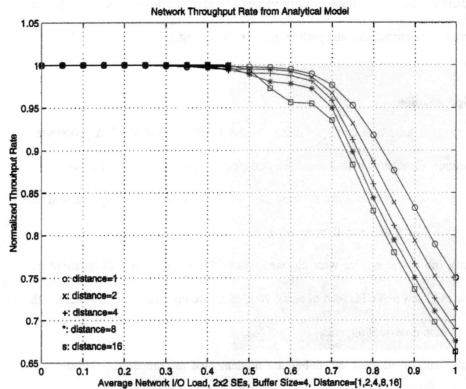

Figure A.1 Estimated network throughput rate using the network performance analytical model in Chapter 4. In this experiment, we use the configuration of *2x2* switch elements, buffer size of *4*, steady-state threshold of *0.001*. The distance between two nodes varies from *1* to *16*, and the system I/O load varies from *0* to *1*.

Locations of resource servers are chosen randomly (uniform distribution). The resources are generated with two parameters: overall size and granularity. A job may need a number, which equals to the granularity value, of resources from servers but the overall size of resources will be constant. In the experiments, there are *6* original resource servers. The average resource granularity of jobs is *3*. Resource servers take *0.05* time units to perform one resource verification transaction. System maintenance messages (e.g. resource validations, jobposts and job assignments) are handled in separate communication channels. Various priority values are assigned to system messages in order to enforce the correctness and performance of scheduling.

A.2 Job Specification

Jobs are generated with two parts using various statistical models: Task processing time is normally distributed with a user specified mean value and a standard deviation of 2. The job generation time interval is 2 time units. This indicates that the system will be saturated with jobs with overall processing time of 98 units in ideal cases. In the experiments, job characteristics were changed from CPU intensive to I/O intensive by altering the I/O loads and CPU load of tasks. 2000 tasks are injected into the system with a total simulation time of 5000 units.

Random and round-robin scheduling are implemented as comparison counterparts. In these two models, there will be no jobpost/bidding processes and, therefore, no bidding overheads are introduced. Jobpost constraint in this experiment is 2 hubs. The deadline for collecting bids in a jobpost/bidding level is 1 time unit.

A.3 Network Configuration

Connection topology determines the number of neighboring nodes and number of communication channels that nodes can use to access resources. In a mesh structure, most nodes have 4 neighbors and channels. A through traffic will generally occupy two channels but without possessing any I/O ports of nodes on the routing path. Augmented network I/O load to these intermediate nodes will be determined by the number of channels occupied by the traffic and by the amount of transmission traffic passing them.

The experiment results were obtained using mesh structure and through network traffic contributed to the network load of the intermediate nodes.

Routes of transmitting resources are determined dynamically in the simulator. It is assumed that a packet stream will travel using the shortest path. In a mesh structure, there are multiple shortest paths. The choice of routing path is determined on single transmission-session basis with uniform distribution over all possible shortest paths. The data communication scheme applied in the simulator is virtual circuit packet switching. That is, all packets in a communication session follow the same route from a source node to a destination node. Packets have to be buffered and queued in intermediate nodes before advancing to next node.

APPENDIX B
EXAMPLE OF OSCULANT JOB PROFILE GENERATION

Example of Function Result Size Table

```
for CNTRL 1 0
remez GEN 1 3 remez
freqz MAX 0.7 1 reduce2
max SAME 0.2 1
flipud SAME 1 1
filter MAX 1 3 filter
cov SAME 0.2 1
randn GEN 1 1 gen
mean SAME 0.1 1
pow SAME 0.1 1 square2
inv SAME 1 1 square
fft SAME 1 1
mul MAX 0.5 2 mul
or MAX 0.1 1
edge SAME 0.9 1 square
size GEN 0 1
```

Example of Osculant Function Profile

```
add -7.68545e-28 6.69121e-23 -1.12671e-18 1 -1.50834e-12
25 81 289 1089 4225 16641 66049
25 81 289 1089 4225 16641 66049

edge 1.56092e-14 -1.46552e-09 3.20962e-05 31.7973 589.345
25 81 289 1089 4225 16641 66049
1396 3164 9766 35258 135400 533060 2115578

fft -8.97307e-12 1.30193e-06 0.012162 220.605 -505.292
25 81 289 1089 4225 16641 66049
2184 8504 80448 251144 1244288 12350024 271991328

mul 6.20275e-11 -2.0626e-06 0.030444 35.2622 -1037.29
1 36 256 1024 3136 7744 16900
1 432 8192 65536 351232 1362944 4394000
```

Function Result Type Table (FRTT) Example

```
Segment of a MATLAB program is shown below:

:                                % IMAGE is an n-by-n matrix
x = mean(IMAGE)'*mean(IMAGE);    % An n-by-1 matrix multiplied by its
```

105

```
            transpose form
   :
x = fft(IMAGE);                    % Take FFT of matrix IMAGE
   :
x = x + 1;                         % Elements of x are increased by 1
     :
```

Estimate of the first reference for variable x is assigned a confidence between 0.1 (mean) and 0.5 (multiplication). The second estimate has a full confidence because of FFT function. The third one has a confidence value of 0.5 because of the operator overload feature in MATLAB. Therefore, the size of variable x will be determined by the second reference. The design of FRTT also allows convenient human knowledge intervention. User experiences can be easily adopted into the profile generator.

APPENDIX C
EXAMPLE OF OSCULANT SIMULATOR USER INTERFACE

```
%        --------------------
%              M A K E . C F G
%        --------------------

% This is a sample of config file which gives the full ability to
% set up an approprate enviroment of simulator.

% All the parameters are idenitically in the name domain. The order
% of the inputs does not affect the simulator. BUT, UNFORTUNATELY
% WE ALLOCATE MEMORY AFTER THE VALUE OF 'NODENUM' AND 'JOBNUM'.
% THEREFORE, WE HAVE TO DEFINE 'JOBNUM' AND 'NODENUM' BEFORE GIVE
% ANY OTHER PARAMETERS. IF WE USE THE DEFAULT 'NODENUM' AND 'JOBNUM'
% WE HAVE TO DECLARE 'DEFAULT NUMBER' AT THE BEGINNING.

%        Use the default job number and node number.
%             Default Number

%        The number of jobs that generated from simulator.
%             Job Number=
                         jobnum.dat

%        The number of nodes that involved in the simulation.
%             Node Number=
                         nodnum.dat

%    Size of cache validation table at resource server
             Cache Table Size=
                         cachetsz.dat

%        Job's resources information. This part of information is
%        quit different from other parts. It requires two parameters
%        The first one is the number of resources, and the second one
%        is the filename which contains the I/O load according to the
%        resources index. The default one is that only one resourrce
%        located at node 41 with I/O load of 40.
             Job Resource I/O=
                         resio.dat

%        The number of cash at each node.
             Cash Number At Each Node=
                         cache.dat

%        Simulation time during which all the results are
%        computed.
             Simulation Time=
                         simtim.dat

%        The time out constrain in the posting algorithm.
%        One can set the time constrain to the total
%        simulation time so that simulator will apply
%        repliable posting algorithm in the 23 bits computers.
%        If one set the time up to a number, the posting will
%        not be accepted after that period of delay.
             Posting Time Constrain=
```

107

```
                    poscons.dat

%         The mutilayer constrain in the posting algorithm.
%         One can set the layer constrain so that no job posting
%         will reach the nodes with a hub distance greater than
%         the layer constrain in one post.
                Posting Layer Constrain=
                        layer.dat


%         Location of jobs. We offer a data file name which
%         contains the location (Node index) of where jobs
%         generated.
%         The file is the location of the the where jobs
%         generated according to the index order of jobs.
%         File data are store in ASCII form.
                Job Location=
                            jobloc.dat


%         Job's generation time. Everything is defined above.
                Job Generated Time=
                            jobgen.dat


%         Job's computation time.
                Job Computation Load=
                            jobcpu.dat


%         Job's memory requirement.
                Job Memory Requirement=
                            jobmem.dat


%         Job's I/O location which we give the main resources
%         index at location where the job's data is located on.
                Job I/O Location=
                            resloc.dat


%         Job's profile size.
                Profile Size=
                            jobprf.dat


%         Node's CPU speed.
                CPU Speed=
                                cpu.dat


%         Node's memory capacity.
                Memory=
                                mem.dat


%         Node's I/O speed (Bandwidth).
                I/O Speed=
                                io.dat


%         Node's local load generator. This file is a
%         little different from others. It offers two
%         parameters of pdf of Gaussian.
                    Local Load=
                                loclod.dat


%         In this file, we supply a masking a logical
%         link matrix. '1' and '0' presents the connection
%         between any two nodes. The connection matrix is
%         a NodeNum by NodeNum matrix.
                Network communication Link Matrix=
                                loglin.dat


%         Physical links between any two nodes which is
%         defined above.
                    Physical Link Matrix=
```

phylin.dat

```
%      Bidding strategies
%           1: Bid_On_Completion_Time
%           2: Bid_On_Utilization_&_Completion_Time
%           3: Random bid
%           4. Round-robin scheduling
%           5. Multiple bid strategy: Dynamic job profile model
%      Future extention: Nodes can apply different bidding strategies and
%                 the strategies can vary in time.
            Bidding Strategy=
                       bidstrgy.dat

            Job Predict Error=
                       jobperr.dat

            Simulated Annealing Auction=
                        simannau.dat

            Node Battery Life Time=
                        batltime.dat
%      Resource Distribution Managament Method
%           1: Plain Method
%           2: Request Frequency Method
              Resource Distribution Management=
                         resdistm.dat


%      Network Load Model
%           0: Point-to-point Model
%           1: Ethernet Model
            Network Load Model=
                        netloadm.dat
```

REFERENCES

[Agarwal 1991]   A. Agarwal. "Limits on Interconnection Network
                    Performance," IEEE Transactions on Parallel and Distributed
                    Systems, Vol. 2, No. 4, Oct. 1991, pp. 398-412.

[Blake 1991]   B.A. Blake, K. Schwan, "Experimental Evaluation of a Real-
                    Time Scheduler for a Multiprocessor System," IEEE
                    Transactions on Software Engineering, Vol. 17, No. 1, Jan.
                    1991, pp. 34-44.

[Bloomer 1996]   J. Blommers, Practical Planning for Network Growth, Prentice
                    Hall, Upper Saddle River, NJ, 1996.

[Chow 1996]   R.Y. Chow and T. Johnson, Distributed Operating Systems and
                    Algorithms, Addison-Wesley, Reading, MA, 1996.

[ComponentWare   "ComponentWare: Component Software for the Enterprise," I-
1997]   Kinetics Inc., Burlington, MA, April 1997.

[Ferguson 1988]   D. Ferguson, Y. Yemini, and C. Nikolaou, "Microeconomic
                    Algorithms for Load Balancing in Distributed Computer
                    Systems," Conference Proceeding, International Conference on
                    Distributed Computing Systems, San Jose, California, June 13-
                    17, 1988, IEEE Computer Society Press, pp. 491-499.

[Gagliano 1995]   R.A. Gagliano, M. Fraser, and M. Schaefer, "Auction,
                    Allocation of Computing Resources," Communication of
                    ACM, Vol. 38, No. 6, June 1995, pp. 88-102.

[Goscinski 1991]   A. Goscinski, Distributed Operating Systems The Logical
                    Design, Addison-Wesley, Reading, MA, 1991.

[Goulde 1997]   M.A. Goulde, "Searching for the Networked Computer,"
                    Patricia Seybold Group, Boston, MA, May 1997.

[Jonhson 1992]   K.L. Johnson, "The Impact of Communication Locality on Large-Scale Multiprocessor Performance," Conference Proceeding, Annual Symposium on Computer Architecture, IEEE Computer Society, Los Alamitos, 1992, pp. 392-402.

[MATLAB 1992]   MATLAB Reference Guide, The Mathworks Inc., Natick, MA, 1992.

[MATLAB 1993]   MATLAB External Interface Guide, The Mathworks Inc., Natick, MA, 1993.

[Ni 1985]   L.M. Ni, C.W. Xu, and T.B. Gendreau, "A Distributed Drafting Algorithm For Load Balancing," IEEE Transactions on Software Engineering, Vol. 11, No. 10, Oct. 1985, pp. 1153-1161.

[Patel 1981]   J.H. Patel, "Performance of Processor-Memory Interconnections for Multiprocessors," IEEE Transactions on Computers, Vol. C-30, No. 10, Oct. 1981, pp. 771-780.

[Park 1989]   C.Y. Park and A.C. Shaw, "Experiments with a Program Timing Tool Based on Source-Level Timing Schema," IEEE Computers, May 1991, pp. 48-57.

[Park 1993]   C.Y. Park, "Predicting Program Execution Times by Analyzing Static and Dynamic Program Paths," Journal of Real-Time Systems, May 1993, pp. 31-62.

[Ramamritham 1989]   K. Ramamritham, J.A. Stankovic, and W. Zhao, "Distributed Scheduling of Task with Deadlines and Resource Requirements," IEEE. Transactions on Computers, Vol. 38, No. 8, August 1989, pp. 1110-1123.

[Ramamritham 1994]   K. Ramamritham, and J.A. Stankovic, "Scheduling Algorithms and Operating Systems Support for Real-Time Systems," Proceeding of IEEE, Vol. 82, No. 1, Jan. 1994, pp. 55-67.

[Rutenbar 1989]   R.A. Rutenbar, "Simulated Annealing Algorithms: An Overview," IEEE Circuit and Device Magazine, January 1989, pp. 19-26.

[Schaller 1997]   R.R. Schaller, "Moore Law: Past, Present, and Future," IEEE Spectrum, June 1997, pp. 53-59.

[Shaw 1989]   A.C. Shaw, "Reasoning About Time in Higher-Level Language Software," IEEE Transactions On Software Engineering, Vol. 15, No. 7, July 1989, pp. 875-889.

[Shin 1988]   K.G. Shin and Y. Chang, "Load Sharing in Distributed Real-time Systems with State Change Broadcasts," IEEE Transactions on Computers, Vol. 38, No. 8, Aug. 1988, pp. 1124-1142.

[Shin 1995]   K.G. Shin and Y. Chang, "A Coordinated Location Policy for Load Sharing in Hypercube-Connected Multicomputers," IEEE Transactions on Computers, Vol. 44, No. 5, May 1995, pp. 669-682.

[Smith 1980]   R.G. Smith, "The Contract Net Protocol: High-level Communication and Control in a Distributed Problem Solver," IEEE Transactions on Computers, Vol. 29, No. 12, Dec. 1980, pp. 1104-1113.

[Stallings 1986]   W. Stallings, Data and Computer Communications, Macmillan Pub. Co. New York, 1986.

[Thomas 1997]   W. Thomas, "Castanet: A New Way to Deliver Software and Content," Netscape Communication Corp., Mountain View, CA, 1997.

[Wu 1997]   H. Wu, C. Chen, and F.J. Taylor, "Osculant: A Multiprocessor Self-Organizing Task Scheduler," Conference Proceeding, IEEE International Performance, Computing and Communications Conference, Phoenix, AZ, Feb. 1997, pp. 35-41.

[Wu 1997]   H. Wu and F.J. Taylor, "Osculant Job Profile Generator: Extracting Job Profile in Source Code Level," HSDAL, Department of Electrical and Computer Engineering, University of Florida, Gainesville, FL, Sep. 1997.

[Yoon 1990]   H. Yoon, K.Y. Lee, and M.T. Liu, "Performance Analysis of Multibuffered Packet-Switching Networks in Multiprocessor Systems," IEEE Transactions on Computers, Vol. 39, No. 3, Mar. 1990, pp. 319-327.

BIOGRAPHICAL SKETCH

Hsin-Ho Wu was born in Taipei, Taiwan, on November 19, 1966. He earned his Bachelor of Science degree in electrical engineering from the Tamkang University in 1989, and his Master of Science degree in electrical and computer engineering from Syracuse University in 1993. He served as an engineering supervisor in the Engineering Corps of Taiwanese Army Force from 1989 to 1991. From 1991 to 1992, he was a teaching assistant in the Department of Electrical Engineering, Tamkang University. From 1995 to 1998, he was a researcher in the High Speed Digital Architecture Laboratory (HSDAL) at the University of Florida. He is scheduled to receive his Doctor of Philosophy degree in December of 1998.

I certify that I have read this study and that in my opinion it conforms to acceptable standards of scholarly presentation and is fully adequate, in scope and quality, as a dissertation for the degree of Doctor of Philosophy.

Fred J. Taylor, Chairman
Professor of Electrical and **Computer Engineering**

I certify that I have read this study and that in my opinion it conforms to acceptable standards of scholarly presentation and is fully adequate, in scope and quality, as a dissertation for the degree of Doctor of Philosophy.

Jose C. Principe
Professor of Electrical and Computer Engineering

I certify that I have read this study and that in my opinion it conforms to acceptable standards of scholarly presentation and is fully adequate, in scope and quality, as a dissertation for the degree of Doctor of Philosophy.

Herman Lam
Associate Professor of Electrical and
  Computer Engineering

I certify that I have read this study and that in my opinion it conforms to acceptable standards of scholarly presentation and is fully adequate, in scope and quality, as a dissertation for the degree of Doctor of Philosophy.

Randy Yuan Chieh Chow
Professor of Computer and
Information Science and Engineering

I certify that I have read this study and that in my opinion it conforms to acceptable standards of scholarly presentation and is fully adequate, in scope and quality, as a dissertation for the degree of Doctor of Philosophy.

Jih-Kwon Peir
Associate Professor of Computer and
Information Science and Engineering

This dissertation was submitted to the Graduate Faculty of the College of Engineering and to the Graduate School and was accepted as partial fulfillment of the requirements for the degree of Doctor of Philosophy.

December 1998

Winfred M. Phillips
Dean, College of Engineering

M. J. Ohanian
Dean, Graduate School

LD
1780
199<u>8</u>

.W95901

www.ingramcontent.com/pod-product-compliance
Lightning Source LLC
Chambersburg PA
CBHW080428060326

40689CB00019B/4419